STUDIES IN
WORLD CIVILIZATION
*Consulting editor:*
Eugene Rice
*Columbia University*

# Latin America: The Early Years

GUILLERMO CÉSPEDES

*University of California, San Diego*

Alfred A. Knopf   New York

THIS IS A BORZOI BOOK
PUBLISHED BY ALFRED A. KNOPF, INC.

*Copyright © 1974 by Guillermo Céspedes*

*Library of Congress Cataloging in Publication Data*

*Céspedes, Guillermo, 1920–*
   *Latin America: the early years.*
   *(Studies in world civilization)*
   *Bibliography: p. 121*
   *1. Latin America—History—To 1600. 2. Latin America—Economic conditions. 3. Latin America—Social conditions. I. Title. II. Series.*
*F1411.C515    918'.03'01    73–17108*
*ISBN 0–394–31810–2*

*Manufactured in the United States of America*

*First Edition*

*9  8  7  6  5  4  3  2*

*Cover design by S. Postow Phillips*
*Cover map by Cardamone Advertising*
*Cover photo by Cyril Morris*

TO  TANA

AND OUR FRIENDSHIP, OUR LOVE,

OUR ADVENTURE IN COMPANIONSHIP.

G.

# Preface

This essay is an attempt to offer a concise and balanced view of the first episode in the Europeanization of the Americas: the founding and consolidation of the earliest modern colonial system. The main protagonists of this endeavor were the Iberians, but important contributions were made by other peoples of Western Europe, West Africa, and—last but not least—the aboriginal Americans.

The subject has been a polemical one since the early sixteenth century. All started with the self-criticism of many Spaniards—the first historical instance of a people submitting to moral scrutiny its own national policies and accomplishments. Accusations by these outraged souls were soon elaborated abroad, mainly in England, as propaganda weapons put to use in religious and political conflicts with Spain. Today, the polemic continues as part of the argument about the virtues of Third World ideologies and the evils of white racism and European imperialism. Our subject has also suffered from many distortions originated by nationalistic viewpoints: history as a way to enhance the glories of a civilizing country, history as instrumental in the building of national mythologies by young nations, and so on.

Nevertheless, the creation of colonial Latin America has uncommon historical interest aside from ideological, ethical, political, and chauvinistic issues. It was not a process of merely local importance, as one may be led to believe by certain books with such a narrow localistic approach (be it national or continental in scope) that, ignoring the Old World, they deprive of all meaning the history of the New. It was not a remote, marginal episode, as it used to appear in the writings of so many Eurocentric historians. It was a phenomenon of world-wide impact, in itself the result of many developments originating outside the Americas, and at the same time a fact that has influenced the course of world history.

The initial period, from 1492 to about 1550, is the most popular and best known. The spectacular accomplishments of discoverers and conquerors possessed strong dramatic appeal, and many books have duly echoed this epic side. Yet those years, closer to medieval than to modern times, may well be considered an end rather than a beginning—the terminal stage of medieval European colonization. We will give them the limited attention they deserve as a transitional, strictly precolonial period.

On the other hand, the century from about 1550 to 1650 was a seminal one in spite of its quiet, unspectacular profile. Developments such as the livestock and crop dispersal, the large-scale production of sugar, and the exploitation of rich silver mines were to originate world-wide economic changes. The pageant of daring explorations was replaced by routine transoceanic sailing; the sober merchant overcame the foolhardy adventurer; remote kings and their quiet colonial officers dethroned arrogant conquerors; the slow but massive Christianization of the Indians was to rival the Reformation in Europe as the last great creative achievement of Christianity.

In his quest for the meaningful and the typical, the student of history must look for a frame of reference and make a choice about what is essential or accidental, important or superficial. Avoiding theoretical questions, let us say that ecological, economic, and social systems (always evolving under the stress of slow change) constitute, in our opinion, a lasting core around which every other aspect of human life must be placed and assessed. To define here this approach as "social," "socioeconomic," "structural," or "total" history, with no room for methodological discussion, would look like mere exercise in semantics. So we will refrain from definitions and concentrate our analysis on the building of new economic structures and the birth of new societies. These elements are important, among other things, because they have proved extremely resilient and durable. In Latin America economic dependence has outlived long-lasting political colonialism. And a patriarcal society has survived the vanishing power of the Church, later trends of secularism, and even the beginnings of religious pluralism.

Social and economic structures were not created out of the blue but were the results of complex processes of transculturation and acculturation, as the anthropologists say. Most of their components were taken from the European, Indian, or African cultural traditions. Some were created anew. Yet the originality of those structures resides in their new functional arrangements of inherited elements rather than in the ones that were invented.

In the best textbooks in the field, it is traditional to deal separately with the Spanish and Portuguese colonizations. The two colonial empires had, of course, very different structures, and no one would dream of comparing them in their entirety. Limiting our attention to the New World, however, there is no doubt that parallel traditions, analogous colonial objectives, and similar situations gave to both colonizations on this side of the Atlantic a remarkable similarity. Moreover, before 1640 the political integration of Spain and Portugal was successively a dynastic project, a realistic possibility, and after 1580 an accomplished fact in the days of Philip II's "Universal Monarchy." The ultimate failure of such a grandiose scheme had far more to do with international power struggles than with alleged deep differences between the Spanish and Portuguese peoples. The treatment of Spanish America and Brazil as unrelated and divergent entities is more a consequence of the historian's specialization in national or regional fields than a historical reality. A new approach is overdue.

This is why we will contemplate the Iberian colonizations as a unified whole, emphasizing their basic similarities (usually forgotten) rather than their episodic differences (often overstated). Regional diversities did indeed appear very soon in colonial Latin America, but to explain them in terms of political boundaries and national European heritages is an anachronism, projecting into the past a recent, exalted form of nationalism that did not exist at the time.

The true reasons for regional diversification should better be found for each area in its pre-European demographic and cultural background, its ecological profile, and its available kinds and amounts of human, technological, and economic resources.

G. C.
*La Jolla, California*

November, 1972

# Contents

# Introduction

Professor Céspedes' stimulating essay about early Latin America is one in a series of twelve paperbacks which Alfred A. Knopf, Inc., is publishing under the title *Studies in World Civilization*. A second essay describes how the principal regions of Latin America won their political independence from Spain and Portugal. Of the ten other studies in the series, one book deals with early and one with modern developments in Africa, China, India, Japan, and the Middle East. The purposes of the series are to introduce students early in their careers to the historical experience of peoples, societies, and civilizations different from their own and to make it easier for teachers of Western Civilization to include in their courses comparative evidence from non-Western history and from the less familiar areas of the Western world.

One of the intellectual virtues of our time is a willingness to recognize both the relativism of our own past and present beliefs and the civilizing value of the study of alien cultures. Yet in practice, as every teaching historian knows, it is immensely difficult to construct a viable course in world history and almost as difficult to include in a satisfactory way unfamiliar, and especially non-Western, materials in the traditional Western Civilization survey course. The reason for this difficulty is that until very recently mankind had no common past. The pre-Columbian civilizations of America attained their splendor in total isolation from the rest of the world. Although the many different ancient peoples living around the Mediterranean were often in close touch with one another, they had little knowledge about civilizations elsewhere. The Chinese knew accurately no other high civilization. Until the nineteenth century, they regarded the ideals of their own culture as normative for the entire world. Medieval Europe, despite fruitful contact with the Islamic world, was a closed society; medieval

Western historians identified their own past with the history of the human race and gave it meaning and value by believing that this past was the expression of a providential plan.

The fifteenth-century European voyages of discovery began a new era in the relations between Europe and the rest of the world. Between 1600 and 1900, Europeans displaced the populations of three other continents, conquered India, partitioned Africa, and decisively influenced the historical development of China and Japan. The expansion of Europe over the world gave Western historians a unifying theme: the story of how the non-Western world became the economic hinterland, political satellite, and technological debtor of Europe. Despite an enormously increased knowledge of the religions, arts and literatures, social structures, and political institutions of non-Western peoples, Western historians wrote a universal history that remained radically provincial. Only their assumptions changed. Before 1500, these assumptions were theological; by the nineteenth century, they were indistinguishable from those of intelligent colonial governors.

The decline of European dominance, the rise to power of hitherto peripheral Western countries such as the United States and the Soviet Union and of non-Western ones such as China and Japan, and the emergence of a world economy and a state-system embracing the planet have all created further options and opened wider perspectives. Historians of the future will be able to write real world history because for good and ill the world has begun to live a single history; and while this makes it no easier than before to understand and write the history of the world's remoter past, contemporary realities and urgencies have widened our curiosity, enlarged our sympathies, and made less provincial our notion of what is relevant to us in our historical inheritances.

Two tactics suggest themselves as viable methods for overcoming the ethnocentric provincialism of an exclusively Western perspective. One approach, especially appropriate in dealing with a non-Western civilization, is comparative history. The comparative procedure has a double advantage.

On the one hand, it describes a culture different from our own and makes clear to us that in order to understand that culture we must scan its history with humility and sophistication, abandoning implicit analogies with our own civilization and leaving aside some of our most fundamental assumptions about time, space, causality, and even about human nature itself. On the other hand, it encourages us to make explicit those very assumptions of our own tradition we now recognize to be different or unique. By studying comparatively an alien civilization we learn something about that civilization—a good in itself—and at the same time sharpen our understanding of ourselves.

A second approach, more appropriate to the history of areas of the world colonized or settled by Europeans, is to study cultural diffusion: how Europe, in the modern period, exported men, ideas, and techniques, to America for example, and how Europeans and Americans attempted to fit them to a new environment and new needs. In this way too we sharpen our awareness of what is distinctive both in the European past and in those societies of European origin transplanted to other continents.

Professor Céspedes' essay on the foundations of Latin American society and culture is both a balanced introduction to early colonial Latin America and a regional history designed to be read in the broader context of Western and world history. It illuminates directly a central problem of European history: the great sixteenth-century price rise. By analyzing the first significant example of a European colonial empire, it helps us understand the nature and causes of the dynamic expansionism that has been so characteristic of European society in modern times. More generally, we will come to understand European culture better by studying its impact on a recipient culture. Professor Céspedes' splendid pages on the family, on the relations of men and women, Europeans and Indians, on religion—to mention only a few of his themes—offer us an excellent opportunity to do so.

Eugene Rice
*Columbia University*

# Latin America:
# The Early Years

# Chapter 1

# The Opening of a New World

The Norsemen were the first Europeans to cross the Atlantic Ocean. Between A.D. 860 and 1001 they sailed to Iceland, Greenland, Newfoundland, Baffin Island, and some coastal tracts of present northeastern Canada, which they probably considered another island in the Atlantic. Their few settlements on this continent were abandoned in 1016 and soon forgotten.

The true expansion of Europe began in quite a different area with the First Crusade in 1096. The Crusaders' kingdoms in Syria and Palestine, lasting from 1099 to 1291, gave the Europeans their first chance to rule non-Europeans. The Italians had known about the whole commercial system between East and West since the thirteenth-century voyages to Asia by Marco Polo and others. But under the shield of the First Crusade Italian merchants (mainly Venetians and Genoans) had their first experiences as colonial traders and settlers in the Middle East and on the coasts of the Black Sea. Venice kept its colonies until the seventeenth century, acting as a middleman in trade between Europe and the Middle East, where Turks and Arabs brought spices and other products from the Far East.

Genoa, less fortunate than Venice, lost its colonies in the eastern Mediterranean at the end of the fifteenth century. Genoans and Aragonese had functioned for a long time as sailors and traders all along the Mediterranean. From 1291 to 1370 they expanded their activities westward, rediscovering the Canary Islands and exploring the Atlantic coast of present Morocco. But their efforts ultimately failed because their galleys, specially constructed for Mediterranean navigation, were unsafe in the open ocean.

Castilian and Portuguese seamen were more successful in overcoming the risks of oceanic sailing. By 1440 they had developed the caravel, a sturdy vessel derived from an outstanding combination of traditional and innovative shipbuilding techniques. Because its motion depended entirely on sails rather than oars, the caravel was able to navigate with the oceanic side winds.

During the fifteenth century Castilian and Portuguese caravels were bitter competitors in the exploration of the western coast of Africa and the eastern Atlantic Ocean. Castilians took hold of the Canary Islands, overpowering the aboriginal inhabitants with the kind of frontier warfare and colonization they had practiced for centuries against the Muslims on Iberian soil. Having established supremacy on the islands, Castilian sailors concentrated on tuna fishing, the small but growing Canary trade, and bartering expeditions along the African coast. The Portuguese did the same elsewhere, but with better results: A weaker Muslim opponent made possible for Portugal a shorter "reconquest" of the mainland and an earlier concentration of resources in navigation and expansion. As a result Portugal secured the Azores and the Madeira and Cape Verde islands, and took a decisive advantage in Africa. The Treaty of Alcaçobas-Toledo (1479–1480) between Portugal and Castile ratified this lion's share for Portugal. Castile, too involved with domestic problems, was able to retain only the Canary Islands.

The immediate Portuguese interest in Africa was in bartering local products (mainly gold, slaves, and ivory) for European weapons and manufactures. But when the Cape of Good Hope was rounded in 1488, the possibility of spice trade with the Orient, quicker by sea and cheaper

4

without the Muslim and Venetian middlemen, became feasible. This goal was indeed accomplished with Vasco da Gama's navigation to India in 1497–1499. Thus Portugal had won both the short- and long-range goals in the competition with Castile.

WESTWARD TO ASIA   The Castilians were left with one risky alternative. Excluded by treaty from Africa and counting on the sphericity of the earth, they attempted to sail westward to the Far East, where no treaty was applicable. Naturally, no ship could undertake such a long journey without having to be resupplied along the way. Several archipelagos were known and many imaginary islands were included in contemporary maps of the Atlantic. With luck an explorer could stumble upon a string of unknown but real islands in time to replenish his supply of fresh water and food. Without such good fortune, his would be a journey of no return.

In 1492 the king of Aragón and his wife, the queen of Castile, decided to risk losing a modest amount of money, three ships, and their crews on just such a journey. Their bet, made against overwhelming odds, partially paid off. Far to the west Christopher Columbus and his Castilian crews discovered a few formerly unknown islands, but more important was their discovery of the proper winds for sailing back across the Atlantic. Asia had not been reached, but the prospects for a second and successful attempt looked good. This remarkable accomplishment is called the discovery of America.

The well-publicized discovery awoke the interest of many sailors and the hopes of some merchants in western Europe. By 1504 a score of daring explorations had made it clear that a hitherto unsuspected, unbroken land mass existed as a formidable barrier between western Europe and the Far East. Vasco Núñez de Balboa crossed the Isthmus of Panama and discovered the Pacific Ocean in 1513, but explorations from the then-impassable waters north of Canada to what is now Argentina in the south failed to reveal an interoceanic passage.

The new land mass had no specific name for a while.

The Spaniards persisted until the eighteenth century in calling it the West Indies. Other Europeans referred to it as the New World. The name "America" was suggested in 1507 in homage to Amerigo Vespucci, a distinguished Italian-born Castilian pilot who was the first to make publicly known the existence of a non-Asiatic fourth continent. The term "America" slowly took hold as the dominant one but has lately been monopolized by the United States. The plural "the Americas" is now emerging as the most accepted term for the north and south continents, whose total separation from Asia was finally corroborated in 1741 when Vitus Bering discovered in the northern part of the continent the strait that bears his name.

Persisting in its initial purpose, Castile found at last the westward route to Asia. In 1519 Ferdinand Magellan embarked with 265 men and supplies enough for two years. For this voyage he used five ships. The expedition, totally organized and financed by the Crown, seems incredibly modern compared with Columbus's first voyage. Roughly thirty-seven months after Magellan's departure, one ship and eighteen exhausted men, with Juan Sebastián Elcano as skipper, reached the port of Seville. After sustaining many casualties and hardships, they had found the long-sought interoceanic passage, now called the Magellan Strait, had crossed the Pacific Ocean, and had circumnavigated the world for the first time. They brought back a cargo of spices that exceeded in market value the total budget of the whole venture. The Castilians had arrived at the Moluccas, the richest of the spice islands, only nine years after the Portuguese.

The Magellan/Elcano expedition could not be repeated without an open conflict between Castile and Portugal—half of the route was in violation of a 1494 agreement by both countries (see p. 101). Therefore a last effort was necessary to find the way back from the Moluccas to America. It was made repeatedly and without success until 1565, when a Spanish ship at last found the right winds and currents for the crossing of the Pacific from the

Philippines to Mexico. But it was too late. The king of Castile, submitting to economic and diplomatic pressures, had given up the spice trade in the 1529 Treaty of Zaragoza. Portugal was again the winner, concentrating all its efforts and resources in the Orient. Castile, excluded from the spice trade, centered all its energies in the New World. This explains why the Spanish colonies in the New World developed and grew much more swiftly than those of the Portuguese.

NEW LANDS, OLD TRADES    Castile's long quest for the spice islands was initiated in 1492 in a joint effort between Columbus and the Crown. The islands were finally reached in 1522 by salaried crews under the exclusive authority of the State. But subsequent explorations of the New World were dominated by private entrepreneurs unaided by the coffers of the Crown. In 1499, navigation to the new lands was open to subjects of the Castilian kingdom. Following medieval commercial tradition, sailors and merchants organized small partnerships in the ports of southwestern Castile for each trip. The sailing partner asked for a permit, or *capitulación*, from the king or his agent in Seville. The *capitulación* was also a contract in which the private partners assumed all the expenses and risks in exchange for royal endorsement and eventual tax exemptions. After the journey was over, the net benefits (if any) were divided among the associates, except for a percentage, usually one-fifth, going to the king. In this way the State stimulated exploration without any risk or expense and eventually participated in the resultant earnings.

The explorers in the New World operated the same way their fifteenth-century predecessors did on the western coast of Africa. When anything of value was found, they merely collected it. This was the case, for example, on the coast of Brazil between the present locations of Natal and Rio de Janeiro, where brazilwood, used as a dye in Europe, was abundant. Since 1502 the king of Portugal had been granting exclusive franchises for such trade, but this monopoly could not be enforced as Spanish, French, and Portu-

7

guese interlopers began to act at will. Applying a course of action used before in Africa against Castilian sailors, ships were dispatched from Lisbon (1516–1530) to attack and exterminate intruders; but Brazil remained an open land, with very few and scattered settlements, until 1549. When collection was no longer feasible, peaceful barter with the aboriginal inhabitants of the coast was tried, again as in Africa. The most fortunate barterers made occasional good strikes. They got pearls and emeralds from the coast of Venezuela and gold from the northern shores of Colombia and Panama. But such business shortly dried up.

Trade could be sustained only with permanent outposts like those established by the Phoenicians and Greeks on the western Mediterranean littoral some two thousand years before. Such coastal settlements could fail and disappear as a result of declining business due to hostility on the part of the natives, or they could prosper and develop into permanent cities if a local, durable source of wealth could be secured. The closest models for these settlements were the Portuguese *feitorias* in Africa, such as Arguim and São Jorge da Mina (later known as Mina or Elmina). These trading posts were at the same time ports, fortified camps, villages, warehouses, and markets. Their role was to obtain and store any available goods that could be sold in Europe at a profit. From time to time they were supplied with weapons, tools, and manufactures for use and barter; these were brought by the same ships that carried the colony's produce to Europe. Thus the sailors soon gave up the risky explorations of earlier days for the more productive and less dangerous regular traffic between new colonies and European ports. In order to minimize expenses and maximize profits, the settlements were supposed to grow their own food and resources and be as self-sufficient as possible. Given the settlers' deep attachment to their nutritional habits, they immediately tried to grow traditional Mediterranean foodstuffs. This was the beginning of a dispersal of European flora and fauna that would originate an economic revolution, first continental and later worldwide in its scope and consequences.

The Spaniards soon established permanent settlements, first on the present island of Haiti, which they duly named Hispaniola (1493) and later on Puerto Rico (1508), Jamaica (1509), and Cuba (1508–1511). The North American mainland was explored around Florida (1519–1538) but not settled until later. On the coast of Venezuela small footholds were consolidated (1509–1535), and the Spaniards also took root in the Darien-Panama area (1509–1514).

The Caribbean settlements were made possible by the early discovery of alluvial gold in the riverbeds of Hispaniola, which spawned the first, albeit modest, gold rush in the Americas. The placer mining techniques immediately applied were demanding neither in capital investment nor in expertise. Pearls and more gold were found in a number of scattered locations throughout the Caribbean area. Although available statistics are not reliable, it is safe to say that a minimum of 14,118 kilograms of legally registered gold reached Seville by 1520. It was gathered from many parts of the Caribbean, but a substantial portion came from the placer mines in Hispaniola. These were practically exhausted by the end of this period, but by then the Caribbean yield had succeeded in doubling the total European production of gold.

**THE FRONTIERSMAN** The first Caribbean gold rush had two immediate and important consequences. First, it stimulated the newly arrived settlers to look everywhere for more deposits of gold, originating a flurry of explorations and new settlements. Second, it created an acute need for abundant manpower in the successful mining camps. The growing trickle of European immigrants was barely enough to provide entrepreneurial cadres, skilled technicians, artisans, and bold adventurers. It never sufficed to fill the large and increasing demand for unskilled workers, who were indispensable for sand washing, construction, food production, and local transportation. Mass immigration from Europe did not materialize, not only because the king tried to limit it to subjects of the Castilian Crown, but also because of a

9

general awareness of the agonies of acclimatization. Unknown tropical illnesses, poisonous plants and animals, humid heat, hurricanes, and the like took a heavy toll in lives and created universal misery among the early settlers. Since most of the Temperate Zone plants imported from Europe failed either to grow or to mature and yield a harvest in that tropical climate, food shortages and high food prices were a general curse. Native food was tried as a last recourse, and in due time an acceptably wide range of mixed aboriginal and imported foodstuffs was selected as the new diet of the veteran residents. But it took years to grow European cattle and develop the earliest Euro-American cuisine, years of painful sequences of expectation and surprise, hope and frustration, achievement and failure.

In short, the European unskilled worker could not be persuaded to move to the new lands for a trifle, and even high wages were not enough to offset dangerous conditions. Another possible source of manpower was slavery, an institution as old as civilization itself. Slavery, however, was in decline at that time in Europe. Slaves still constituted about 10 percent or more of the total population of certain areas in southern Portugal and Castile. Some slaves were brought to the Caribbean, but the cost of acquisition and transportation was almost prohibitive for the Spanish pioneers. (The Castilians, having lost direct access to the sources of African slave trade, had to pay onerous prices to Portuguese middlemen.)

The sweet, peace-loving Arawak Indians of the Greater Antilles became the easiest and least expensive solution to the manpower problem. Most of the gold had been found within their territory. The Arawaks welcomed the Europeans, probably because they were afraid of the Carib Indians (then expanding across the Lesser Antilles and literally eating the Arawaks up) and hoped to get help from the newcomers. The latter, on the contrary, soon asked the Arawaks to help them with sand washing and other daily chores. The Arawaks refused. Living as they were in a subsistence economy, they considered it utterly crazy to work hard for the sole purpose of gathering gold, that good-for-nothing yellow stuff. The Spaniards, immersed in a monetary economy, concluded that the Arawaks were lazy, barbarian, and perhaps even subhuman. They proceeded to set up a general allocation of Arawak manpower to the mining business. They naturally considered this to be in the public interest because it made possible honest earnings for the Christian community and tax revenue for the king. The customary tragic chain of events unfolded quickly: anger on the part of Indians forced to work for no "logical" purpose; massacres of settlers, and rebellions that were ruthlessly crushed, with slavery as punishment for the survivors. The virulent spread of European diseases was the final blow to the Arawaks. They practically disappeared before the Caribs had the opportunity to eat them all.

By 1504 some Spanish settlers had expressed their revulsion at such a state of affairs. The queen had declared illegal the enslavement of Indians on the basis of solid medieval traditions, both moral and legal: The only legitimate sources of slavery had always been war against the infidels or honest purchase, and the heathen were to be enslaved only if they had initiated an aggressive, unjustified war against the Christians. This latter point was enough to provide the Spaniards with a loophole for paying lip service to law and justice without discarding their only solution to the manpower shortage. As soon as the natives of Hispaniola were decimated, other Indians were imported from neighboring islands. Prospectors and barterers who failed elsewhere in their search for gold could always round up a cargo of Indians, bring them to Hispaniola (or any other prosperous mining area), and sell them as slaves. They would say, of course, that the Indians had attacked them while peacefully trading or prospecting, therefore these Indians were legal slaves as prisoners taken in "defensive" war. Slave manpower was so welcome that nobody believed an Indian who protested—even in the event of his being understood.

The new business boomed. Ruined entrepreneurs, unscrupulous adventurers, poor sailors, and all kinds of pursuers of quick, easy money organized *compañas* or *compañías*, small business partnerships with the explicit purpose of prospecting for gold or carrying on any other respectable activity. In practice they selected their field of action from the areas most densely populated by peaceful Indians. They soon learned that every business has its hazards when even the gentlest Indians became determined fighters. The slavehunters then did two things. One was to try to obtain slaves through peaceful barter with Indian groups willing to sell them; the other was to organize themselves into efficient military groups. Their raids were often successful, thanks to their growing expertise in such matters. Their tactics and organization closely followed traditional models of frontier warfare practiced for centuries in medieval Iberia by Muslims and Christians alike. The slavehunters' experience and growing familiarity with the environment gradually neutralized the initial advantages enjoyed by the Indians in their defensive fighting. Furthermore, the European raiders made devastating use of their technical superiority: The horse gave them mobility, speed, and wide operating range; the shepherd's dog, duly trained, made it possible to avoid ambushes and track down and terrorize Indians; and their traditional steel weapons, mainly swords and shields, were far more effective than firearms, which were scarce, expensive, and easily ruined by rust in the humid tropics.

Spanish *compañías* were active in many Caribbean islands (1508–1515), in Darien-Panama (1510–1531), in northern Colombia (1526–1535), and in Venezuela (1529–1544) which was sometimes under German leadership. But they gradually gave way to quieter, more humane ways of life. Although these groups started as slavehunters, many of them, on purpose or by accident, discovered mines, opened the way for regular settlement, and charted unknown territories. They even tried to uncover remote, rich Indian empires, sometimes illusory, like El Dorado, sometimes real, like the Aztec and Inca civilizations. In short, they were the advance party of Europeanization. They forged themselves into the best possible tools for the conquest of America. Their know-how, audacity, and endurance enabled them to adapt to exotic lands and foods, meet unforeseen dangers, and survive climates that newcomers from Europe could not endure. Despised or feared by many, these *baquianos,* or veterans of the Caribbean world, earned at least the respect of some, and later became the backbone of every successful conquest. The best *baquianos* succeeded from a combination of outstanding personal qualities, good opportunities, and sheer luck. They became ambitious, stubborn leaders, ready to risk their lives for money, social prestige, and political power. A handful attained some or even all of their goals; most died in the endeavor.

The frontier of the *baquianos* was soon exhausted, but another appeared elsewhere. The Brazilian *bandeiras* were from 1506 to 1690 the Portuguese counterpart of the former Spanish *compañas.* They undertook the same sort of slavehunting and slave-bartering expeditions to the inland, then went back to the coast to sell captive Indians as slaves for the sugar plantations, and finally returned home to São Paulo or elsewhere. The range of the *bandeiras* was longer and their movements slower than those of the *compañas.* The profile of the former was more a product of racial and cultural miscegenation. Many *bandeirantes,* or members of a *bandeira,* were half-breeds. Their weapons consisted of bows and arrows rather than swords and it was more common to see them walking than on horseback. But they, too, were explorers, discoverers of mines, and the vanguard of Europeanization, and they must be counted among the founders of Brazil.

THE CONQUEROR
AND
HIS HERITAGE

The Spaniards were ready for a large-scale occupation of the continent only twenty-five years after their arrival in the Caribbean. Between 1516 and 1518 the settlers of Cuba had gathered enough resources and information to use their island as a springboard for the conquest of Mexico. Under the brilliant leadership of Hernán Cortés, they destroyed the Aztec Confederation (1519–1522) and occupied central and most of southern Mexico. Present

Guatemala and El Salvador were under their control by 1524. It took more time to defeat the Maya Indians of Yucatan, but by 1543 this region too had been seized. The whole area was baptized New Spain—a clear testimony to the conquerors' relief when they reached the temperate Mexican plateau after years of hard life in tropical lowlands. The territorial expansion of New Spain was stopped by the wilderness in northern Mexico and by another group of Spaniards coming from Panama in the south. The clash between the two groups accounted for most of the violence in the early settlement of Central America.

Panama, as we have just indicated, was the starting point for the other great Latin American conquest: the vast domain of the Incas, henceforth known as Peru, the Hispanicized version of an Indian name for a river located in the area. After a long decade of painful exploration, magnificent stubbornness on the part of Francisco Pizarro, and the incredible endurance of his companions, the core of the Inca empire was reached and overcome (1532–1533). However, the years of conquest were not over until 1537, when a great Indian revolt was suppressed. A neo-Inca state barely survived until 1572 in the mountain refuge of Vilcabamba, but it was never a challenge to European rule.

From Peru the conquerors moved north to Quito, in present Ecuador, and into present Central Colombia, meeting on the plateau of Bogotá other Spaniards coming from the northern coasts of Colombia and Venezuela. Peruvian expansion to the east succeeded in partially occupying the Bolivian Plateau but failed to penetrate beyond that point after several spectacular explorations of the Amazon River and its basin. To the south, a small cluster of settlements was established in central Chile. These had to face not only long-lasting resistance from the Araucanian Indians but also the isolation imposed by the Atacama Desert to the north and the Andean mountain range to the east.

Beyond the early Spanish Main and the territories covered by the Central Mexican, Mayan, Chibcha, and Incan civilizations, Spanish attempts at colonization met with little success. Failure was total in Florida until 1565, and almost total in Buenos Aires, which was abandoned soon after its founding in 1536. A remote settlement near Asunción, Paraguay, subsisted in isolation until 1580, when a new generation of half-breed settlers was able to reestablish Buenos Aires as their port for communication with Spain (see Map).

No doubt the extension and profile of the conquest was strictly predetermined by the geographic location and cultural level of the aboriginal peoples. Wherever sophisticated Indian civilizations existed, conquest was quick and effective. In such areas the Spaniards inherited the concentration of power formerly in the hands of the Indian military, political, and religious elites whom they had fought and destroyed. They took advantage of the available economic surplus, as well as a dense population accustomed to organized work, in order to build and equip their new colonial settlements without disturbing the existing social and economic structures. When dealing with simpler civilizations —cultivators with small economic surplus, weak political organization, and low population density—conquest and colonization occurred more slowly owing to Indian resistance, poor economic prospects for the conquerors, or a combination of both. This is why Portuguese Brazil developed so precariously during the first half of the sixteenth century. Wherever the aborigines were nomadic, the population sparse, and the economy at strictly subsistence level, Iberian colonization either failed, was not attempted at all, or ended as soon as deposits of precious metals were exhausted. In short, the outcome of all attempts at colonization depended on the cultural gaps between Indians and Iberians. The narrower the gap, the greater the speed and success of colonization; the wider the gap, the larger the possibility of failure. Colonization of an unusually difficult or unfavorable location was carried on at high cost and only when the strategic or economic value of that location fully justified the effort. But such efforts generally took place only after the period of conquest.

It seems paradoxical, given their large professional armies

and vast resources, that the highest aboriginal civilizations, such as the Aztec and Incan, were so quickly and totally defeated. The Spaniards, fighting on unfamiliar terrain in bands never stronger than a few hundred men, always short of key war supplies, were nonetheless the winners. This cannot be explained solely in terms of bravery and determination. Brave and determined they were, of course, but their opponents were not exactly cowards themselves. The conquest can be explained partially in terms of European technical superiority. War horses, dogs, steel weapons, and firearms were totally unknown to the Indians, as was their tactical use. The Indians were quick to learn about them, but they learned too late. Long and effective resistance was possible only when the Indians had both the time and the opportunity to borrow war techniques and weapons from the enemy, as was the case with the Araucanians. Horses and vessels gave the Spaniards a logistic superiority and a capacity for reinforcement and long-distance communication that the Indians could never match, especially at sea.

Important differences in cultural traditions also granted the Europeans positive advantages. War, though always a contest of strength, had different meanings, functions, and rhythms in the Old World than in the New. For the Aztecs war was just a way to obtain tribute and prisoners; for the Incas it was connected with religious rituals. In contrast with these more limited and partly ceremonial concepts of war, the Spaniards practiced a "total war" that never left room for any outcome other than either full victory or death. For the Indians a parley with the Spaniards was a diplomatic ritual; for the conquerors it meant a golden opportunity to capture the enemy chief and use him as a hostage, following ancient Old World practice.

Religion had considerable weight in psychological attitudes toward war. The Spaniards' was a militant, crusading, aggressive religiosity. Their ancestors had seen St. James fighting on their side, eagerly killing Moors in critical battles of the Reconquest; the conquerors in the New World also saw St. James, this time charging against the

Indians. Unlike the optimistic, morale-building attitude of the Christians, some aboriginal religions cultivated the somber concept of life as a cycle of growth and decay, splendor and doom. The Indian elites were sometimes overcome by their own apprehensions and were always shocked by unexpected, "illogical" actions or reactions on the part of their enemies. In due course they had to admit that their gods had been defeated and that the invaders, backed by their true and almighty God, were unbeatable.

Finally, the most effective instruments of conquest were the Indians themselves. The Spaniards easily recruited Indian informers, interpreters, spies, guides, and even loyal advisers and committed allies. Many natives considered the newcomers' rule preferable to that of the existing elite. Indian social and political systems had their share of rebels and nonconformists, alienated and oppressed peoples, as well as mere opportunists ready to side with the probable winner. This was the case, for example, with the Tlaxcalan Indians, who were understandably fed up with their long oppression by the Aztecs. The Spaniards made good use of such attitudes and resentments because they badly needed all the help they could get. Without willing and decisive Indian assistance, the conquest could have taken long centuries instead of short years, as happened in certain regions such as Chile.

For the conquerors defeat would have meant either death or bankruptcy. They made the conquests at their own risk and expense, according to the terms of *capitulaciones* that specified the legalities of each enterprise. The king granted his permission to conquer a territory within a given period of time. He appointed the group leader as his officer, stated his royal right to part of the booty (as established in medieval Castilian war laws), and promised rewards to the conquerors in accordance with their future merits and services. No wonder complaints were voiced about the scanty contributions of the Crown, which were generally limited to *papel y buenas palabras*, "a piece of paper and a few promises." The conquerors were supposed to procure their own equipment and supplies, fight hard, and win. In cases of failure they took care of their wounds, losses, expenses, and debts as well as they could, only the dead being free of further problems. Customary statements about the greed and cruelty of the conquerors must be evaluated in light of their frequently disastrous financial condition and the many kill-or-be-killed situations they faced.

War booty was exceptionally high in only a few cases and small or insignificant in many others. Substantial rewards were expected only after a successful conquest, in the form of royal mercies. Knowing that the Castilian nobility had been created during the Middle Ages in recognition of military services against the Moors, the conquerors tried since 1519 to portray their heroic deeds as glorious political endeavors, national in character and religious in ultimate purpose. From Hernán Cortés on, they claimed to fight for God and king, expanding the Crown's dominions and paving the way for expansion of the "true" faith. For doing this they felt that they deserved the same (if not better) prize the heroes of the medieval Reconquest had obtained—that is, access to the ranks of the nobility. The Castilian nobles considered the conquerors to be pretentious upstarts, their hands red with Indian blood and their gold of suspect origin. The word *indiano*, coined in Spain and applied to everybody coming back rich from the Indies, had a derogatory connotation. Hence only a small handful of great conquerors, whose accomplishments could not be minimized or ignored, received titles of nobility. A number of them were rewarded with appointments to the royal bureaucracy and served until death or dismissal in the territories they had conquered. The office of governor was the most prominent of these positions.

In theory these governors had limited political authority that the king could revoke at any time. In practice, however, the leaders of the conquest could not be deprived of their trophies. Their personal prestige, enhanced by the title of governor, allowed them to rule for the benefit of themselves and their companions. Some of them spent their energies and even their lives in bloody disputes with former associates; the War of Salinas in Peru (1537–1538) and Francisco Pizarro's assassination in 1541 are typical examples of this. Others were gradually deprived of political power by the encroachment of professional bureaucrats sent by the king. This was the case with Hernán Cortés, who spent his last years in Spain a rich man, mature and intelligent enough to care more for peace than for games of power. But as a group these conqueror-governors ruled long enough to build their own world and to leave a lasting impact on colonial society.

Their political ideal was a feudal society totally medieval in profile. They tried to perpetuate their powerful hold through their sons and successors, as in a feudal military aristocracy. As vassals to the king of Castile, their duty after the conquest was to defend, rule, and keep peace in their territories. For such purposes, they remodeled an old Castilian institution, the encomienda, which the Crown had tried to transplant since 1512 to the Caribbean with the intention of moderating somewhat the brutality of the system of compulsory labor formerly imposed upon the Indians. Starting with Cortés in New Spain, encomiendas were granted to the conquerors in order to make them "lords of vassals," the vassals being the aboriginal inhabitants of the conquered territory. Encomienda was a system by which each prominent conqueror obtained from his governor a large number of Indians, with authority to rule them and exact from them a tribute in goods and services. The tribute had to be large enough to provide for the needs and duties of the *encomendero*, or beneficiary of the encomienda. These "necessities" included a good aristocratic living for himself, his family, and his retinue of friends, relatives, dependents, employees (among them one or several stewards), servants, and guests; a mansion house; enough horses and weapons to equip himself and the males in his retinue in the event of an emergency; and the means to keep peace, administer justice in his fief, and pay instructors to teach the Indian vassals how to be good Christians and "civilized" men. The king as supreme lord, the governor as his representative, and the *encomenderos* as loyal vassals of the king were the "nerves and bones" of a feudal political society where, as in a human body, the noblest parts have a privileged ruling mission to fulfill and the whole is perfect and harmonious.

This ideal was never reached because the *encomenderos* went against the grain of political trends and realities in Castile. The Crown was progressing in its attempt to create a modern, centralized state after curbing the political power of the nobility, and the king could not tolerate the emergence of a new feudal aristocracy overseas. A sector of the clergy sided with the king for ethical reasons, trying to defend the Indians against the *encomenderos'* greed. The conflict culminated in the issue of succession to the encomiendas. The *encomenderos* wanted succession to be purely hereditary; the Dominican friars, as self-appointed defenders of the Indians, wanted encomiendas entirely abolished on moral grounds; and the Crown, less radical but more effective than the friars, tolerated the system for a time while successfully undermining it. Encomiendas were confirmed by the king for the life span of its beneficiary and only reluctantly extended to one or more successors.

The principle of perpetuity was never accepted; gradually royal officers were sent to the colonies to take over the political and judicial authority of the *encomenderos*. These officers still respected the economic rights of encomienda because the tribute of the Indians was declared a royal tax ceded to the *encomenderos*. However, in 1542 the encomienda and all forms of Indian slavery were abolished. A general uproar—including open rebellion in Peru—forced the suspension and later the softening of such a radical solution. Thus the encomienda survived, but only as an economic institution deprived of all the political meaning intended by the conquerors since 1519.

The alliance of Crown and Church, plus the lack of any solid ideological and political support in Castile, were strong factors against the consolidation of feudalism in the Spanish colonies. But perhaps the main reason for the system's failure was the inherent weakness of the conquerors as a political group. To govern and organize a territory, to succeed as public administrators and as founders of feudal dynasties proved even more difficult for them than conquering those lands in the first place. The conquerors, recruited mainly from the ranks of commoners and the impoverished lowest echelon of the nobility, lacked the education and training needed for efficient statesmanship. Beneath their external adoption of aristocratic ways of life, they felt a certain lack of self-confidence. Some of them even sold, in disguised form, their encomiendas. They preferred to enjoy the worry-free life of rich commoners in Spain than to face the responsibilities of feudal lords and the demanding task of creating a ruling elite in America. Political pressure from the Crown denied them the time to learn their new jobs and to fully develop their self-consciousness as a ruling group. An effective, self-confident, and self-perpetuating political elite cannot be improvised.

Though *encomenderos* failed to retain any political power, their role as founders of new but tradition-oriented societies had a lasting impact. Their military accomplishments earned them fantastic prestige in the colonies, in spite of their social origins and considerable lack of social acceptance in Castile. As successful, brave, self-made men, they were shown full respect at the local level and formed the top stratum of early colonial society. Although they were somewhat ostentatious, prodigal, and boastful, (perhaps to compensate for inner feelings of insecurity after "making it" too quickly), they adopted with good grace the aristocratic styles suited to their new role. Cultivating dignity, pride, and generosity, they set up a durable pattern of patriarchy that survived for a long time in Spanish-American social elites.

The early *encomenderos* were numerically a small group, comprising the upper crust of the society of the conquest; the main body of that society consisted of humbler Spaniards. Most of the latter never dreamed of entering the *encomendero* elite because they had fought in the conquest without special distinction, lacked the ambition or taste for it, or had arrived too late, when the fight was over and the prizes already granted. Others never intended to participate in the conquest—they included merchants, sailors who decided to stay in the colonies, artisans who went there in order to make more money in their trades and became employers instead of employees, and latecomers of all kinds. Very soon they had settled in small urban clusters. A few, however, spent a long time in rural areas, which were then totally Indian. Among them were travelers, missionaries, prospectors, stewards, and other employees of the *encomenderos*; others were poor shepherds who cared for the first European livestock introduced to the New World. The farmers in charge of the agricultural holdings, generally close to the city, were usually urban dwellers.

The city soon crystallized as a microcosm fully Castilian in structure and profile but with original traits of its own. The local elite consisted of a few *encomenderos*. Small groups of priests, physicians, titled and untitled lawyers, and public notaries began to coalesce into an incipient middle group. From here on down the social ladder, merchants and artisans of all trades, as well as servants and slaves, formed the permanent core of the city. The slaves, working as artisans or domestic servants, came in small numbers from Spain with their masters. They were either African blacks or Muslims from Spain or North Africa who had already been Hispanicized. An unstable group of transients included visiting merchants, peddlers, new immigrants not yet settled, adventurers, and the usual vagrants. A growing number of uprooted Indians, early collaborators of the conquerors, settled in the cities as employees, artisans, servants, and unskilled laborers, and were promptly Hispanicized by social pressure. Other Indians soon came with their families, voluntarily or otherwise, to toil in the building and other urban trades. They created dwellings on the city outskirts, the first functional precedent of later proletarian slums. The Indian element gave a typically American trait to otherwise Castilian cities. The female population, too, was new in its composition: Spanish women were few at this time; there were many more Indian females, living with their families in the slums or as wives, mistresses, or servants of the Spaniards. However, as in most new settlements, women were in the minority.

A pale counterpart of the Spanish conquest took place in Brazil in 1533–1549. The concentration of Portuguese resources in the Far East and the absence of high aboriginal civilizations in Brazil made the beginnings of colonization there slow, difficult, and uncertain. An organized plan to develop a net of permanent settlements was not seriously contemplated until 1530. The king of Portugal finally decided to apply to Brazil the same medieval system of colonization formerly practiced on the Madeira Islands. The Brazilian coast was divided into fifteen captaincies granted to lord-proprietors. These lords and a formal charter provided the ingredients for a purely feudal regime in each captaincy. The project was a total failure because the lords were unable to gather enough human and economic resources to sustain the settlements. In 1549 Brazil consisted of two prosperous clusters of sugar cane plantations in Pernambuco and São Vicente, and practically nothing else.

# Chapter 2

# Economic
# Structures

F rom the 1520s to the 1550s, the cities of New Spain
and Peru progressed far on their way to self-sufficiency. The
temperate areas in which these cities were located were more
attractive to emigrating Castilians than the Caribbean
tropical lowlands had been. At last there were enough
entrepreneurs and skilled workers in all trades arriving in
the New World. Mediterranean flora and fauna were
introduced wherever possible. A large and self-supporting
Indian population provided all the unskilled (and mostly
unpaid) manpower needed for building and general production in the new settlements. An economic surplus,
consisting mainly of gold until 1530, provided for a few
vital imports like iron products and a number of luxury
items such as fine clothing, wines, and olive oil. This early
transatlantic trade was a windfall for Castile, which increased its agricultural and industrial production for export
overseas.

EXPORT SECTOR:  The boom was kept within the territorial limits of the
PRECIOUS METALS  kingdom until the 1550s, when a sudden, drastic economic
change took place. Big silver mines were discovered at
Potosí (1545) and Zacatecas (1546) (see Map). In only

twenty years, from 1545 to 1565, all the major mining strikes in the Mexican plateau and the central Andes were made. Silver was an easy commodity to carry. Because of its high value, the cost of its transatlantic transportation could be met, and it found a strong, immediate demand in the Old World for use in silverware, jewels, and other luxuries. It was also used for monetary purposes. Europe, relatively well supplied with gold at the time, was short of silver: In the early sixteenth century the price ratio of gold to silver was 1:10.11—that is, silver had a relatively high price.

These circumstances soon transformed the late-medieval Spanish colonies on this continent from modest but well-balanced, increasingly diversified economies into capitalistic, highly specialized, unbalanced, export-oriented economies producing mainly for European markets. This economic dependence, the true origin of the later and much-lamented Latin American economic "underdevelopment" (actually unbalanced development), was to last for centuries.

The newly discovered mines yielded silver ore requiring a rather complex metallurgy, quite expensive and elaborate compared with Caribbean gold placer mining. Colonial metallic exports were 100 percent gold until 1530 and about 85 percent silver from 1530 to 1560; silver would later amount to almost 98 percent of the total. This meant that investment in silver production was heavy; in fact, the Crown stimulated such investment by cutting the traditional rate of taxation from 20 to 10 percent. At first the silver ore was reduced by oxidation. However, owing to the scarcity of firewood and other fuels in the mining regions, this created critical transportation problems. To solve these problems Bartolomé Medina, a resident of New Spain, invented in 1555 a metallurgy of amalgamation: He mixed ground silver ore with mercury, salt, and several other substances; then, by means of careful washing and final distillation, pure silver was separated and a large part of the mercury recovered for further use. The new technique, soon introduced in Peru (1572), cut fuel consumption drastically, since fire was necessary only for the distillation of the silver-mercury amalgam and the casting of silver in bars. However, it required mercury—rare, expensive, and difficult to transport without leakage. A barely adequate container was developed in the form of a strong wooden crate lined with leather.

In an effort to minimize the distances it had to be transported, mercury was actively sought in the silver-mining areas. Only one big deposit was found (1563). This deposit, located in Huancavelica, Peru, was a blessing for fiscal purposes: Mercury production and traffic were then organized as a state monopoly to provide a source of tax revenue and a means of controlling and stimulating silver production. Huancavelica provided about 75 percent of all the mercury required for silver production in the New World. The rest, up to a long-term average of 370,000 kilograms per year in 1561–1660, came from the mine of Almadén, Spain, while Idria, a mine in present northeastern Italy but at the time within the Austrian dominions, remedied episodic shortages.

The initial mining camps soon developed into full-fledged cities. Potosí, for instance, was located in a desolate, cold area 13,780 feet above sea level, creating fantastic problems of settlement, transportation, and supply. Everything alive had to undergo a difficult process of acclimatization. This included men (the town later had over 160,000 inhabitants), animals (such as the many mules and horses essential for transportation), and plants (most of which failed to thrive). Potosí yielded only silver —about half the world production in 1546–1601—and everything needed for this came from long distances in pack trains: European tools and manufactures, cattle and leather from northern Argentina, mercury from Huancavelica, foodstuffs from Peru and Chile.

The problems encountered in the Mexican mining region were less severe, because manpower could be brought from shorter distances. Moreover, food could be produced and livestock bred locally, eventually to a point close to self-sufficiency. But the wealth generated in this way was a temptation for the nomadic Chichimeca Indians of the north. In order to secure the area against their raids, it was necessary to create frontier settlements manned by missionaries and military garrisons. The zeal of the former, the aggressiveness of the latter, and the discovery of more silver mines to the north all contributed to the gradual but steady advance of this frontier through a combination of diplomacy, purchase, religious conversion, and sometimes war. The Chichimecas came under control and the area was settled by about 1600. And as a bonus the Spaniards obtained the necessary experience to create a mission system that was to serve them well in later territorial expansion as far as the present American Southwest.

Silver mining always required high investments and large amounts of manpower. The technicians and skilled workers were well-paid Europeans, their ranks soon reinforced at the lower levels by half-breeds and Indians. They did the mining and built shafts, galleries, and water power systems (over thirty reservoirs were built in Potosí). The water power was used to operate mills (over one hundred in Potosí) in which the ore was ground. When not enough water was available, the mills were kept in motion by cattle. All of these tasks were preliminary to the metallurgical process, a complex and tedious set of operations that culminated with the melting of silver bars. The many indispensable unskilled workers were drafted Indians periodically sent to the mines with their families for variable lengths of time. Their recruitment was organized in the manner of the pre-European system of temporary forced labor formerly imposed on the Indian communities for military or public works. In the Inca realm it had the Quechua name of *mita* (shift). Both the name and the institution survived in colonial Peru with some alterations, the main difference being that the work was paid for in colonial currency instead of goods.

Part of the silver produced in the colonies remained there either as raw material for jewelers or as currency. Peruvian silver was coined at the royal mint of Potosí, established in

1572; in New Spain the silver was sent to the mint of Mexico City, created in 1535. The rest was exported in the form of silver bars. The bars were carried from Potosí to the port of Arica by pack trains and from there to El Callao, the port of Lima, by sea. From El Callao to Panama all the Peruvian exports were transported in a convoy of ships under military protection. In Panama the cargoes were carried across the isthmus to the Caribbean port of Nombre de Dios, later replaced by Portobello.

The Mexican silver followed a shorter route, from the northern mines to Mexico City and the port of Veracruz, going by pack train all the way. After 1543 the crossing of the Atlantic was made once a year in a convoy of ships with military protection. The convoy sailed from Seville, where the *Casa de Contratación,* or royal Board of Trade, organized the sailing and collected export taxes. In 1564 the system was changed in order to avoid bad weather, minimize ship losses, and facilitate the dispatch of the fleets: The convoy for South America left Seville in March, the one for Mexico in June; only a few small vessels with royal orders and mail were dispatched during the rest of the year.

When the convoys reached Portobello or Veracruz, the Peruvian or Mexican merchants, respectively, were waiting with their silver. A short but hectic fair was held, and then the colonial merchants went back to Lima or Mexico with European merchandise and the convoy, after a stop in Havana, sailed back to Europe with Peruvian and Mexican silver. The production of New Granada (present Colombia), mainly gold, was collected in the port of Cartagena, where a smaller fair was held. All the vessels, including a few from lesser Caribbean ports, were resupplied and regrouped in Havana before sailing back to Seville.

The key to this commercial system was the short fairs in Portobello, Veracruz, and Cartagena; colonial merchants and European cargoes were supposed to reach these cities simultaneously. This required complex planning—not always successful—at both ends of the route. Even a short delay meant a great increase in expenses for merchants and freighters, as well as health hazards for passengers not accustomed to life in the tropics.

The silver route did not end at Seville. In a matter of days the silver consigned to the king was sent to the court in Madrid, whence it was soon sent to the Netherlands, northern Italy and Rome, Germany, and the rest of central and western Europe to cover loans, interest, and the military, diplomatic, and political expenses of the Crown. Some of the silver kept by the merchants was coined as Castilian currency. But both coins and bars soon ended in Medina del Campo, where they fed an international fair. From there the silver soon found its way to the rest of Europe, compensating for an increasingly adverse balance of trade and divergent bimetallic ratios. This was accomplished both legally (export licenses were easily obtained from the 1560s on) and illegally (smuggling was rampant, though its extent is impossible to estimate). Aside from the contraband subtracted at each step of the commercial system, a minimum of 16,985,000 kilograms of legally registered silver reached Seville between 1531 and 1660. Of this total, 15 percent arrived in 1531–1580, 67 percent in 1581–1630, and 17 percent in 1631–1660; the greatest influx came during the decade from 1591 to 1600. During the same period some 155,000 kilograms of American gold reached Seville by legal means. Although it is risky to correlate these figures to the total stock of precious metals in Europe, it is tentatively estimated that American imports increased the European stock of gold and silver by 20 percent and 300 percent, respectively, during those years.

The economic impact of such imports was great but difficult to evaluate even today. One consequence was that the price ratio of gold to silver changed from 1:10.11 in 1503 to 1:14.84 in 1660. As a result the economic relationship between Europe and the rest of the world was drastically altered. Since silver was scarcer and hence more expensive in the Far East, European merchants and rich men could pay with American silver for more oriental goods, thereby stimulating imports from Asia. How much silver went to the Orient we do not know, but it seems that certain Asian markets were occasionally glutted with silver during the seventeenth century. In this way America made possible a quick development of world trade, which benefited primarily the European middlemen: merchants, bankers, shipbuilders, and industrialists. Nevertheless, a large but undetermined quantity of precious metals remained in Europe; much of it was put to noneconomic uses, making possible the splendid Baroque decoration of architectural interiors, sculpture, jewelry, clothing for the rich, and innumerable samples of workmanship by goldsmiths and silversmiths. The remaining bullion was coined, greatly increasing the monetary stock of Europe and influencing its economic development.

As early as 1556 Spanish writers related the higher cost of living in Castile to imports of American bullion. The "revolution" in prices gradually spread over Europe and, according to the traditional explanation, inflated the profits of merchants and manufacturers, encouraging industrial growth and capital formation. (Costs and wages grew too, but, as is typical, at a slower pace.) American bullion has thus been blamed for the rise of capitalism. But the correct interpretation is more complicated. The fivefold rise in average European prices during the sixteenth century, doubtless a shock to societies used to relatively stable prices, had many causes. These included demographic factors such as population pressure; economic causes like wars and poor harvests; and monetary reasons, including not only the increase in the monetary stock but also changes in the bimetallic ratio and national fiscal policies leading to inflation and debasement of currencies. Yet in spite of all these qualifications, the fact remains that American bullion deeply influenced the economic evolution of Europe and the world. It bolstered the upward push in prices and capital accumulation in Europe; it created a large market in the Spanish Indies for European products and manufactures, thereby stimulating production and industrial development in Europe; it encouraged European emigration overseas, originating in this way the first stage of a gradual Europeanization of the New World. If the rise of capitalism actually antedates the discovery of America, there is no doubt that American bullion, and the transoceanic trade it stimulated, accelerated the process.

The transatlantic trade fluctuated, however. The years 1503–1550 witnessed a sustained increase, but the total volume of traffic was comparatively modest and affected mainly Castile, fed by Caribbean gold and the economic surpluses of the conquest period. In 1550–1562 a plateau was reached. The impact of Peruvian and Mexican silver was small, probably because colonial investment in the development of the mining areas and the commercial system was heavy and gave limited surplus. After 1562, transatlantic trade rose quickly, reaching its highest point in 1581–1630. The full impact of silver production was felt, while the colonial market for European products reached its maximum. From the 1620s on, a steady decline took place, becoming serious after 1650. The silver boom was over, and the colonies appear to have participated in the seventeenth-century European depression. This point will be discussed later in this chapter.

The building up of the silver business required as much energy, ingenuity, daring, and entrepreneurship as the conquest had demanded years before. Its working elements were unskilled Indian manpower and European technicians and entrepreneurs. These miners, industrious but poor individuals frequently forming very small companies, depended entirely on credits and loans. Their only sources of financing were the merchants, who could provide expensive supplies and advance large sums. The whole mining and commercial structure had a cyclical yearly rhythm. During most of the year the miners received loans from the merchants. These were paid back, with interest, at the time of the fairs, when the merchants needed all their capital for acquisition of European merchandise. As the merchants sold their imported goods they received cash, and this was loaned to the miners until the next fair. The cycle was repeated year after year. A competent, honest miner usually made a good living with hard work, and a few became very rich men. As soon as they were reasonably well off they usually retired, investing their hard-earned money in land or other low-risk, less demanding economic activities.

The largest portion of the mining profits went to the merchants in their capacity as suppliers and bankers: When they financed successful mining ventures they got the lion's share, whereas in the event of failure the miner was ruined and had to start again from scratch; the merchant could recoup his loss out of commercial profits. In this way a small number of successful colonial merchants were able to gather the large amounts of capital and credit indispensable for participation in the fairs of Portobello and Veracruz. The concentration of economic resources required by this system favored oligopolistic and monopolistic practices, which led to high prices, large profits for a few merchants, high risks and moderate earnings for mining entrepreneurs, good wages for skilled workers, and subsistence income for the many unskilled Indian laborers involved in the mining and commercial system.

**EXPORT SECTOR: TROPICAL CROPS** The typical early specialization of colonial exports had several causes. First, trade could consist only of goods that Europe was unable to produce or did not produce in quantity—provided that sufficient steady demand for such goods was maintained in European markets. Second, trade was limited by the high cost of transatlantic transportation to goods of high value and relatively small bulk. Third, demand for American products had to be built up—Europeans did not immediately develop a taste for formerly unknown items like cocoa, cotton, and tobacco, though they would later become eager consumers of these products. And fourth, colonial exports could not materialize until production sufficiently exceeded local consumption. Consequently the hides that provided the raw material for leather manufactures essential in mining, transportation, and footwear were exported relatively late and in small amounts, in spite of the fantastic proliferation of European livestock in the virgin pastures of the New World.

To offset these limitations, one factor helped diversify the Spanish-American trade: the large difference in volume between European exports, some fairly bulky and moderately priced (such as wine and olive oil), and colonial silver, high in value but low in bulk. Thus less tonnage was required for the voyage from the colonies to Europe than for the return trip. Although some vessels were sold in Caribbean ports for intercolonial trade and others, corroded by tropical woodboring molluscs, were abandoned there, it was always feasible—and marginally profitable—to load products instead of ballast in ships bound for Spain. Such was the case of cochineal, a Mexican insect that was dried and ground to produce a convenient red dye used mainly for silk textiles. Indigo, a blue vegetal dye, was also exported from Central America and Mexico. Toward 1570 hides became the bulkiest Mexican export and the most valuable Cuban one; during the seventeenth century they were the key export from Buenos Aires. A variety of medicinal plants from the whole Caribbean area were early and steadily exported, but in small amounts. Among these, tobacco proved to be the most important: Sixteenth-century physicians prescribed it for about fifty illnesses (including asthma) with the same crusading enthusiasm their modern counterparts exert in proving its lethal qualities. Addiction on the part of their patients ensured the success of tobacco in Europe and elsewhere. And when an adequate form of packaging was designed to counteract the propensity of tobacco to absorb shipboard odors, large-scale trade became feasible. The Spanish fleets carried sizable cargoes of tobacco from the early seventeenth century on, and Brazilian tobacco exports reached about 1,250 tons per year in 1610. (Meanwhile the contraband between Venezuela and Europe was developed by Portuguese interlopers.) In 1620 the Spanish Crown introduced a state tobacco monopoly that became very productive and continues to flourish today in Spain.

Sugar was the first tropical crop to be developed as a big business. In the late European Middle Ages it was produced in small subtropical areas of the Mediterranean basin and considered a rare, expensive drug. The Iberians brought it to the Atlantic archipelagos, where it did well with artificial irrigation, especially on Madeira. The Spaniards brought sugar cane to America from the Canary Islands. By 1530 there were commercial plantations in Hispaniola, where some twenty years later there were forty sugar mills in operation. Sugar plantations (*ingenios azucareros*) soon appeared in the Mexican lowlands and as far south as the Peruvian coast. Sugar quickly entered the Spanish colonial diet in unprecedented amounts; therefore most of the crop was consumed in the colonies. By the sixteenth century only Hispaniola, Puerto Rico, and some Mexican plantations conveniently close to Veracruz exported sugar to Spain. Large local consumption, lack of investment capital (monopolized by mining), high costs of production (African slaves were expensive), and inadequate marketing in Europe were the main factors keeping down Spanish sugar exports until competition with Brazil was no longer possible.

Brazil enjoyed all the advantages for sugar cane agriculture. First, there was a strip of excellent black and red soil along the coast from Pernambuco (now Recife) in the north to São Vicente (near present Santos) in the south. Second, adequate rainfall made artificial watering unnecessary, rendering cultivation less expensive than on the Atlantic islands. Third, there were many ports close to the sugar fields, making it easy to export sugar to Europe; Pernambuco and Bahia were soon the most active of these. Fourth, a marketing organization already existed at the end of the fifteenth century for the sugar from Madeira, including partners, sources of credit, and facilities in Antwerp for distribution of sugar throughout Europe. And last but not least, the Crown adopted toward the sugar business an open-handed, liberal policy, the only available means of developing its Brazilian colony.

Two serious problems remained: the need for investment capital and the lack of abundant manpower. Capital came freely from the Netherlands via partnerships between planters in Brazil and Dutch merchants in Europe. Manpower was initially recruited on the spot in the form of forced Indian labor; this being insufficient, the *bandeirantes*, flouting the passionate but useless protests of the early Jesuit missionaries, brought Indian slaves from the interior. Eventually additional and better manpower was obtained from the western African coast, then under Portuguese control, in the form of black slaves. Thus was inaugurated the transatlantic slave trade: Soon black slaves were coming to Brazil in large and growing numbers. Low taxation, temporary tax exemptions, and virtually free trade further enhanced the Brazilian sugar boom.

Once the jungle had been cleared and the sugar cane planted, it grew splendidly with a minimum of care and was ready to be cut in about six months. Each plant could be harvested several times, provided that it was allowed to grow after each cut. It took time for the fertile soil to be exhausted, and when this point was reached the land could simply be abandoned and the jungle permitted to grow again; plenty of virgin land was available for further clearing and seeding. However, while sugar cane growing was easy in Brazil, processing and transportation required heavy investment. The cut cane was taken to a sugar mill and the juice it yielded carefully processed in wood-burning boilers and allowed to crystallize in molds. Then the sugar was dried, purified, and crated in big wooden chests weighing about 500 kilograms each. Two grades were produced for export: crystalline white and brown, the latter to be refined in the Netherlands. The first mills, in São Vicente (1533) and Pernambuco (1542), each yielded approximately 50 tons of sugar per year and were operated by about six skilled workers and twenty unskilled slaves. A minimum of twenty oxen were required to haul cane, firewood, and sugar crates if the mill was water driven; if it was driven by oxen or mules, up to sixty head of cattle were needed.

The sugar mills grew steadily in size and number, stimulated by growing European demand and increasing productivity; soon most mills required several hundred men. In 1570, Brazilian sugar was already a big business, with 60 mills producing about 2,500 tons per year, and in 1600 some 120 mills yielded about 30,000 tons. Between 1608 and 1612 a new type of mill with vertical cylinders was brought from Peru and quickly adopted throughout Brazil because of its higher efficiency. From 1630 to 1654 the Dutch occupation of northern Brazil disrupted Portuguese sugar production, but in general did not reduce exports: Though Portuguese mills were destroyed or abandoned in the north, new ones were established in the south, mainly in the region of Rio de Janeiro, while the Dutch did their best to continue the intensive exploitation of the area they occupied. The peak of Brazilian sugar exports was reached between 1629 (with 346 mills in operation) and 1660, and was accompanied by the highest sugar prices. The latter were partly due to monetary inflation, but in a buyer's market in which Europe was both the consumer and the provider of capital investment, the level of prices was determined by European factors and did not have a decisive effect on Brazilian production and profits. In fact, the planters' profits were always reduced by high payments on loans. In 1660, therefore, in spite of ever-growing European demand, the Brazilian quasimonopoly of sugar production ended. Exports, prices, and benefits were gradually but steadily eroded by competition with new Caribbean plantations. There the Dutch, English, and French planters would prove in due course their ability to outsell and outproduce the Portuguese, in spite of a new Brazilian technique for boiling the sugar juice (1656) that cut by two-thirds the amount of firewood required. This was the last technological innovation in the Brazilian sugar industry before the nineteenth century.

Nevertheless, Brazil was the first Latin American region to fully develop a new socioeconomic structure: the sugar plantation. This evolved during the seventeenth century and consisted of several square miles of sugar fields, grazing areas for cattle, woodlots for firewood, a large house for the master, a chapel, living quarters for employees and slaves, barns for the cattle, warehouses for foodstuffs and processed sugar, a carpentry shop for carts and crates, a smithy for repairs and toolmaking, a workshop for sugar processing, and the sugar mill—which soon gave its name, *engenho de açucar*, to the whole plantation. The *engenho*, a peculiar mixture of capitalistic exploitation and patriarchal society, and a slow melting pot for African, Iberian, and Amerindian races and civilizations, was soon copied (with eventual variations) by the rest of tropical America—first in the Lesser Antilles, later in the southern English colonies of North America, and finally in nineteenth-century Spanish Cuba.

Brazilian sugar originated a commercial system far more flexible and less well-organized than the Spanish system. Portuguese ships sometimes sailed from Lisbon to Africa, where they bartered their cargoes for slaves to bring to Brazil. In fact, direct trade between Brazil and Angola was important enough so that Angola seemed occasionally to depend more on Brazil than on Portugal. Navigation between Brazil and Spanish Buenos Aires as well as land trade between southern Spanish and Portuguese territories, though mostly illegal, was customary in the seventeenth century. Efforts were made to dispatch the sugar cargoes in convoys from Brazil to Portugal, but these were not very successful before 1649, and so many ships were exempted from convoy sailing that the exceptions outnumbered the rule. Unlike the Spanish Seville, Lisbon was not the only metropolitan Portuguese port for colonial trade. Moreover, it was often feasible to sail directly from Brazil to the Netherlands without stopping in Portugal. This loose organization was due only partially to the inefficiency of the Portuguese royal bureaucracy and the relatively liberal policy of the Crown. The main reason was the total economic specialization in sugar that made early Brazil, like the Atlantic archipelagos, a peripheral sector of the western European economy. As we will see, the Spanish-American colonies developed their seventeenth-century production enough to cover a large part of their needs. Brazil, by contrast, relied entirely on imported goods. Although the *engenhos* grew some garden vegetables and fruits, all their human resources were devoted to sugar production, and most of the daily food of masters and slaves alike came from abroad. Since Brazilian livestock did not prosper until the 1640s, most meat was imported; tools and manufactures, of course, were also imported. Brazilian sugar was the first economic monoculture in the New World.

The consequences of the sugar trade, though less spectacular than those of the silver trade, were important and far-reaching. Brazil transformed sugar from a marginal commodity produced in small amounts at high prices into a basic element of the human diet produced in huge quantities at moderate prices. As an ingredient in confectionery, fruit preserves, and many other recipes, sugar was enjoyed by rich Europeans as a delicacy and gradually filtered down to humbler and poorer levels of European societies. Portugal, as middleman, derived from the sugar trade sizable profits which made Brazil the economic center of the Portuguese empire when most of the colonies in the Far East were lost. But a price is always paid for progress, and just as the benefits of silver production were paid for by the Amerindians with the tragedy of forced labor in the mines of Peru, those rendered by Brazilian sugar were paid for by Africans and Amerindians with the abhorrent revival of slavery and expansion of the slave trade. As is usually the case, those who skimmed the profits were not the ones who suffered the exploitation.

THE DOMESTIC SECTOR

We have seen how the Brazilian export sector was developed in tropical coastal regions close to Europe and open to easy, direct sea traffic with the outer world. This required only a few city seaports as nodes of traffic and distribution. On the other hand the Spanish-American cities, built near the silver mines, were located in remote, scattered, temperate inland zones, difficult to reach and far from the Atlantic. Direct sailing from the Pacific coast of South America to Europe was possible, but too dangerous and time-consuming for commercial navigation before the eighteenth century. The Spaniards, then, had to create an extended economic infrastructure of agriculture, cattle raising, and industrial production, as well as long traffic routes from the mines to the Atlantic ports. To supply this vast structure with imports only—as the Portuguese did in Brazil before 1650 —would have required a volume of transatlantic transportation that simply could not be afforded. This is why the ideal of a self-contained, self-sufficient economy inherited from the period of the Spanish conquest was never abandoned during colonial times.

The Portuguese export system was fully developed by about 1630, when the sugar trade reached its peak. For the sake of brevity we will bypass the then-minuscule Brazilian domestic sector, which was fed almost exclusively with imports until 1650. At that time Brazil was basically a coastal monoculture related to (and supplemented by) the frontier economy of the *bandeirantes*. The Spanish export system, by contrast, was created with almost incredible speed despite fantastic geographic obstacles: It was fully grown by about 1580, when the peak of silver exports was reached—roughly half a century before the Portuguese system was fully developed.

While the Portuguese established predominantly rural settlements in Brazil, the Spaniards settled in cities from the beginning of the colonial period. They did so for several good reasons. First was security: In the event of Indian rebellions, they could survive only in groups, the larger the better. Second was politics: An isolated Spaniard could accomplish nothing. But a group of legal residents of a "city" constituted a Castilian community with political rights, including the rights to petition the king, to appoint a solicitor or lobbyist to the Court, and to govern themselves as a municipal entity. A third reason was self-sufficiency: In a large enough group it was easier to find people of all trades and abilities.

Late in the sixteenth century the Spanish colonial cities could be grouped into three basic economic categories:

1. Agricultural cities, many founded during the conquest period and hence relatively old. Such cities were located in the midst of dense Indian populations which provided through *encomienda* enough supplies and manpower for the urban settle-

ment and its residents. Some were established on the sites of former Indian cities (Cuzco), others built on the ruins of such cities (Mexico City), and still others created anew (Lima).

2. Commercial cities located at key points on sea or land trade routes. The importance of these cities as markets (Cartagena), ports (Havana), or relay points (Arica) depended on the volume and wealth of the traffic they handled.

3. Mining cities, whose birth, progress, and decline depended entirely on the yields of neighboring mines (as was the case in the Lake Titicaca region).

A number of cities belonged to two or even three of these categories and were consequently the most prosperous. Others soon increased in importance by becoming centers of political and religious power at either the regional (viceroyalties, archbishoprics) or the provincial level (governorships, bishoprics). Similarly, the proximity of manpower and raw materials transformed other cities (like Puebla) into cores of industrial production for colonial markets. Finally, some urban settlements prospered along inland routes as centers of vast cattle-raising regions (Córdoba, Tucumán) providing meat and transportation for the whole system.

Until 1630 the Spanish-American cities increased considerably in both number and size. The number of Spanish colonial cities has been estimated at 225 in 1580 and 331 in 1630. During these years their size increased, on the average, more than threefold, from a hypothetical total of about 460,000 urban dwellers in 1580 to some 1,500,000 in 1630. (These figures may be taken as valid indicators but not statistical realities. The number of inhabitants represents the total of households multiplied by twenty. This gives an estimated total for the Spanish households but does not include the growing Indian districts on the outskirts of the cities, which were the first urban ghettos in the New World.) In any case the trends of urban growth and migration from rural areas to cities are clearly as old as the Spanish colonization and typical of a process of expansion undertaken with limited resources in a vast space. Such trends are even more remarkable if we consider that they took place in a period during which the Indian population declined sharply:

By about 1630 the trend toward urban concentration had begun to slow, probably because the demographic reserves of the extensive zones influenced by the cities were totally exhausted. From then on urban settlements grew slowly or remained stagnant, and compensatory migrations from urban to rural areas took place. Another meaningful fact is that the urban population tended to concentrate more and more in large cities, as shown in the following figures (note the qualifications stated earlier): The percentage of the total urban population living in cities with over 10,000 inhabitants of all races in Spanish households was 40 percent in 1580 and 75 percent in 1630; the rest of the urban population lived in smaller cities—60 percent in 1580 and only 25 percent in 1630.

Thus the first Latin American urban boom was over shortly before the end of the period covered here. Let us now evaluate its main typical traits. The amount of resources invested in the whole endeavor cannot be quantified because statistical sources are lacking; it is therefore impossible to determine what percentages of the total economic output of early Spanish America were devoted to colonial development and exploitation by Spain. Nevertheless, it is safe to say that, in contrast to Brazil, the Spanish colonies were far more than an economic fringe of Europe. Toward 1580 they were self-sufficient in agricultural production—even olive trees and vineyards had been grown in many places. As we have seen, modest amounts of tropical crops were consistently exported to Europe. Livestock production also left a sizable surplus, making possible exports of hides and later of tallow. Moreover, a determined effort had been made to develop an import-substitution industry: leather products and cotton and wool textiles manufactured in sweatshops operated with Indian manpower, as well as manufactures of all kinds produced by artisans in small and medium-sized shops. The Crown initially stimulated diversified colonial production in order to favor development and thus accelerate mining production. Later, however, its policy was to stop this diversification so as to maximize colonial economic dependence on the parent country. The former policy was as great a success as the latter was a total failure. The seventeenth-century Spanish colonies imported only two essential metals (iron and mercury). The remaining imports were luxury items with a limited market among the rich.

The centers of economic development were, indeed, the silver mines working largely for the export sector. The mining zones naturally generated considerable interregional trade in the colonies, and areas which were satellite economic entities, supplying the mining regions and their commercial export system, were extended. The colonial cities managed to capture a considerable percentage of the silver production for their use and consequently were able to meet their own economic needs. Although intercolonial trade was either forbidden by the Crown or, after 1604, limited to the bare minimum, this policy failed completely because diversity of climates and production favored interregional commerce. Illegal trade among Pacific ports, from Acapulco in the north to El Callao in the south, always flourished; contraband between Brazil and Venezuela was rampant; and two-way smuggling between Brazil and Buenos Aires, and from there to Potosí, was a persistent scandal in which respectable merchants and governors were involved. More than a matter of corruption and venality, generalized intercolonial contraband was a product of spontaneous colonial economic development versus an unnatural, restrictive economic policy that obviously could not be enforced.

An unknown but considerable part of colonial exports to and imports from the Old World escaped the legal framework devised by the Crown. From Havana to Buenos Aires the Atlantic colonial ports traded illegally with Dutch, English, and French smugglers. After 1571 the Manila galleon (dispatched once a year to supply the handful of Spanish missions and settlements in the Philippine Islands) was the cover for a sizable contraband that carried American silver from Acapulco as far as China and brought back Oriental silk, porcelain, and other luxury manufactures to Mexico City, Lima, and many ports along the Pacific coast of the Spanish Indies. The contraband was paid for with local produce, silver bars, or the excellent Spanish colonial currency (not coined for export but exported nonetheless). The peso, whose value remained remarkably stable until 1686, was very much appreciated in Europe for its high silver content. This was also the case in Asia and in all the non-Spanish colonies of the New World, where Spanish colonial silver coins soon came into general use. The peso's broad diffusion throughout three continents proves that the Spanish-American economy had a strength of its own far beyond the legal limitations imposed by the king.

In the light of these facts, let us evaluate the seventeenth-century economic depression. If it existed in Europe it was due primarily to European causes: wars, poor harvests, epidemics, a slowdown of demographic and economic growth. On the other hand Europe seemed to need less American silver than before, partly thanks to better and wider credit facilities, partly owing to the falling value of silver in terms of gold as a consequence of the growing stock of silver. The decreasing European demand for silver, compounded with the increasing economic self-sufficiency of Spanish America, were good enough reasons for the decline in transatlantic trade. Thus the colonies absorbed the unfavorable impact of a European slowdown.

The colonies had their own problems, however. The most serious was the precipitous decline of the Indian population, a possible source of critical manpower shortages. Silver production was also adversely affected by the scarcity of mercury in New Spain (due to diminishing and less regular transatlantic trade) and growing metallurgical problems everywhere. Higher production costs appeared as soon as more accessible veins of silver ore had been exhausted.

These colonial problems, in turn, tended to aggravate the situation in Europe and contributed to the depression there. Or so the generally accepted explanation goes.

There is no doubt that New Spain was the region most severely affected by this downward trend, but the question remains as to whether it was a merely regional phenomenon or a general one. In the case of Brazil we have seen how the first half of the century was a period of economic expansion. For the rest of the colonies there are no clear-cut answers. In general terms, however, whatever economic slowdown occurred was far less serious than the decline in legal transatlantic trade would lead one to believe. Colonial traffic in Seville was seriously affected by deadly local epidemics in 1599–1600 and 1649–1651, by the economic short-sightedness of local merchants, and even more by frequent royal confiscations of silver remittances for private individuals, mostly merchants. This desperate trick of bankrupt kings struggling to pay for their military and dynastic policies in Europe positively discouraged traffic through Seville. As a result merchants resorted more and more to smuggling in amounts that are unknown but certainly became larger and larger; a contemporary guess put smuggling at 50 percent of the legal trade—a fivefold increase of contraband in the middle decades of the seventeenth century.

If the contraband in Europe is added to the growing illicit trade of the Spanish colonies with the Philippines, Brazil, and every foreign smuggler who cared to sail to Spanish Caribbean ports, there is reason to believe that the total economic output of the colonies did not decrease. Moreover, the viceroys gradually held back more money for administrative and military expenses overseas, sending in consequence less and less to Spain. If we put together all these factors, it could very well be that, despite regional exceptions, the seventeenth-century economic depression never reached the Ibero-American colonies as a whole. By about 1650, while redirecting their external commerce, the colonies seemed to be slowly expanding and modestly broadening their economies.

MARGINAL AREAS   The integration of the Indians into a European type of economy was a gradual process with as many variations as there are regions and climates in Latin America; historical circumstances also contributed to the variety. Where aboriginal cultures were highly developed, the degree and speed of integration depended mainly on the proximity of the Indian groups to colonial cities. In the cities Indian residents (even temporary forced labor) were quickly integrated into a monetary economy. In the adjacent rural areas the spread of encomienda gradually forced Indian communities to participate in the colonial economy, first by giving part of their crops as tribute, later by cultivating European crops for tribute payments, and finally by raising commercial crops, which they sold in order to pay the tribute in cash. In remote areas of difficult access, however, Indian groups were willing and able to preserve their traditional production and economic life. But sooner or later they learned and adopted, at least partially and selectively, new farming techniques, European livestock, plants brought from other American regions and from Europe, and a number of alien crafts. The main factors forbidding or delaying these innovations were either ecological (such as the failure of imported plants to adjust to local climates or the lack of raw materials for a given craft) or psychological (as in the case of deliberate rejection, which was possible if a community was large and sufficiently isolated to preserve its cultural traditions). Paradoxically, the Indians who resisted the Europeans longest were Iberianized sooner and more thoroughly than those who were easily overcome. In order to resist they had to adopt the technology of their enemies, thereby opening the door for a revolution in Indian economies. The neo-Inca state in Vilcabamba and the Araucanians in Chile are outstanding examples.

Where the aboriginal cultures were less developed, economic assimilation was slower and more difficult. Missions and frontier settlements were the focal points for the spread of European farming and technology. Even where they were successful, however, it took a long time to break the closed economic systems of these areas and to prepare them, through the raising of commercial crops, for the adoption of a monetary economy. In some areas, including many Caribbean islands, colonization resulted not in assimilation but in total extinction of the aborigines.

In any case, a European type of economy spread gradually outward—like an oil spot—from each developing colonial city. Wherever the colonists were able to exercise some influence, economic integration into the colonial system was accomplished to a greater or lesser degree. Sooner or later even the remotest Indian group had a tribute to pay and something to bring to market for profitable sale or barter. Rather than speaking of several economic systems in colonial territories (such as monetary, non-monetary, and subsistence economies), one should refer to an ever-expanding economic structure of commercial capitalism in different stages of development.

The only marginal areas were those never reached by colonial expansion—the poorest and least populated ones. But even these felt the impact of European colonization. For example, the Tehuelche Indians of Patagonia began to use horses before coming into direct contact with white men. Horses made it possible for these nomadic hunters to drastically change and improve their technique. To the north horses ranged far beyond the Mexican frontier, transforming the lives of many Indian groups before their first contact with Europeans. On the other hand there is evidence that epidemics of European origin, transmitted by long-distance Indian trade, ravaged the population of certain regions long before the arrival of the first colonist.

# Chapter 3

# Social Structures

The total population of the American continent on the eve of the European conquest is unknown. It is estimated that there were at least 80 million Indians, very irregularly distributed. About one-fifth of these Indians, living in North America and marginal areas of South America, had practically no contact whatever with white men before 1650. This leaves some 64 million natives in territories subject to Iberian colonization. The most populous region was Central Mexico, with 20 million people or more controlled mainly by the Aztec Confederation. The second largest group lived in the central Andes under Inca rule; its size has been estimated at between 3 and 32 million people and was probably closer to 7 million. Smaller demographic concentrations inhabited the Chibcha cultural area of present Colombia (almost one million people), some of the Caribbean islands (Hispaniola is supposed to have had over 3 million inhabitants), and the northern part of Central America (with about 800,000). In addition, there were minor clusters scattered through certain zones of Brazil, Chile, and Venezuela. Other regions were sparsely populated, if at all.

POPULATION AND
IMMIGRATION

Population growth in pre-European times resulted from the right combination of good climates, rich soils, and Indian civilizations with well-developed agricultural technology (improved seeds, irrigation, terracing, and the like). Human populations, like those of all living species, tend to grow to the limit of available resources. The point of overpopulation is reached sooner or later, and the resulting crisis is solved either by a more or less catastrophic demographic decrease or by technological breakthroughs that increase productivity. The years 700–1000, for example, witnessed a number of crises in nuclear America that meant the end or at least the transformation of the classical civilizations. The deepest causes seem to have been ecological ones: loss of productive soil through exhaustion and erosion, food shortages, epidemics, and violent conflicts among neighboring peoples competing for land, water, and other resources needed for food production.

In the last pre-European historical period, appropriately named the Militarist period, political and military power became concentrated in the hands of aggressive elites that ruthlessly exploited the richest agricultural regions and subdued their populations. War as a permanent instrument of policy, massive sacrifices of prisoners, and extended use of platforms of mud and aquatic plants built out into lakes are symptomatic of the cheapness of human life and the scarcity of productive soil in the valley of Mexico before the arrival of the Spaniards. The admirable Maya civilization disintegrated before the Europeans came to Mesoamerica. Massive resettlements of human groups in the Andes, usually explained in terms of imperial Inca expansion, probably also represented emigrations of land-hungry peasants from overpopulated areas. And in Central Mexico the ecological balance was so unfavorable and overpopulation so critical that a disaster could have been expected in the sixteenth century even without the advent of the conquerors.

Overpopulation and ecological deterioration in the New World motivated periodic compensatory demographic decreases before the arrival of the conquerors. In some regions the presence of the Europeans did nothing more than accelerate these cyclical processes. This happened on such a scale, however, that it produced a demographic disaster without counterpart in the history of mankind. Mexico is the best-documented instance: A population estimated at over 20 million in 1519 was reduced to 16.8 million in 1532, 2.6 million in 1568, and 1,069,255 in 1608. A modest recovery did not get under way until the 1650s. In certain areas the decline was steeper than in others. In the Mexican coastal regions the depopulation ratio for the years 1519 and 1568 was 47.8 to 1, while in the Mexican plateau it was 6.6 to 1. Moreover, it has been estimated that 3.7 million Indians lived in Hispaniola in 1496; only 250 remained in 1540. In many of the Lesser Antilles, the Indians were totally eliminated, though this happened later under non-Iberian rule.

The Caribbean islands are an extreme case, and Mexico undoubtedly follows as the most serious instance of depopulation in both degree and speed. Other areas have not been studied as systematically as Mexico, but a comparable pattern emerges everywhere: quick and extensive depopulation in tropical coastal lowlands, with considerably lower losses on temperate inland plateaus. The demographic decline was slower elsewhere than in Mexico. In Peru, for instance, the low point was reached in the eighteenth century, and the subsequent recovery was a slow one.

Even if some of the estimates just given are exaggerated, the size and general trend of this demographic loss is beyond dispute. The causes were many, but war must not be counted among them: The conquest was short, and colonial rule meant a period of relative peace and stability compared with earlier times; thus in demographic terms the impact of war was almost nil. More important were the effects of the many migrations caused by the presence of the Europeans and their prodigal use of Indian manpower. Native communities moved to remote and poorer lands to avoid the conquerors; tribute payments, which were out of control for a while, probably deprived the Indians of a major part of their production; in addition, many natives were taken from the fields to build cities, roads, and ports. Moreover, the temporary allocations of Indian groups for all kinds of public works (or any work considered to be in the public interest) was a wasteful system producing unskilled, careless gangs of workers who spent most of the time walking back and forth from their homes to their working places in frequent shifts. Indian migrations to the cities (voluntary or otherwise) also decimated or wiped out large units of formerly active cultivators; food production must have declined in consequence.

The expansion of European livestock did the rest. In Central Mexico alone over 29,000 square miles were granted (mainly to Spaniards) as pasture lands. In the long run this favored the Indians, who were replaced by cattle in doing transportation work and received meat to supplement their almost meatless diet, but in the short run the growing herds of cattle roaming free destroyed many cultivated plots before they could be harvested. In addition, sheep and goats overgrazed the soil, especially in arid and semiarid lands, provoking erosion and creating extended badlands. From the 1550s on the situation was aggravated by the expansion of the mining industries, which took a very large amount of manpower formerly devoted to agriculture. The raising of tropical crops for export had similar consequences.

The Iberians could have done something to remedy the resulting decline in food production—and did so from the 1570s on—but they could do nothing to neutralize the biggest cause of Indian depopulation: infectious diseases brought from the Old World. Viruses and bacteria had traveled throughout Europe, Asia, and Africa as a result of migrations, wars, and long-distance trade, with its sequel of deadly epidemics, but the impact of many diseases had been felt over millenia and the groups affected had time to recover their demographic losses and develop resistance. The Amerindians, however, having lived hitherto in practically total isolation, felt in the span of a few decades the compound impact of all the diseases that could be spread by European ships and their passengers and cargoes. Lethal factors moved in both directions, however—Europe suffered outbreaks of American syphilis, among other things. But the formerly isolated Indians were the big losers: Epidemics of smallpox, typhus, measles, and influenza, relatively mild among self-immunized Europeans, had horrible effects on the Amerindians, increasing their mortality rate. It has taken roughly four centuries for them to fully recover in absolute numbers from the demographic loss suffered in the sixteenth century. Tropical America, which had been relatively healthy, was almost depopulated by malaria, yellow fever, trachoma, and other diseases that have remained endemic until very recent times. It is poor consolation to know that much later, in Australia and the islands of the Pacific, similar circumstances had similar demographic effects, even though the mechanisms of infectious disease transmission were already known and some vaccines had been developed.

The Amerindian demographic losses were only partially compensated by immigration. The existing records on white immigrants are fragmentary, and total figures are unknown. However, the European population of Brazil has been estimated at 3,500 for 1550, 35,000 for 1600, and 70,000 for 1650. The Spanish colonies may have received 100,000 immigrants in the sixteenth century and somewhat fewer in the seventeenth. They were mainly Castilians, but immigrants from other kingdoms of the Spanish Crown, technically foreigners in Castilian territories, came to the colonies in small numbers. Portuguese immigrants also settled in the Spanish colonies, mainly between 1580 and 1630. In addition, other foreigners such as Genoans, Germans, and Greeks were present from the days of the conquest in very small numbers, mainly as merchants, technicians, and illegal immigrants; they were soon totally assimilated into the dominant Spanish or Portuguese stock. Jews of several national origins also came, though not many, and there were an unknown number of recently Christianized Jews among the immigrants, mainly in Brazil, and also in the Spanish colonies in spite of legal prohibitions. In sum, European immigration was far from massive in the colonial period. Only 1 percent of the total population in 1570 was white, but as a result of high reproduction rates and immigration this figure rose to an estimated 6.3 percent by 1650.

The high cost and dangers of transatlantic sailing discouraged many prospective travelers and kept down the number of passengers. The conquest of Mexico and Peru was the first serious incentive for emigrants; when this had been accomplished, both the character and the flow of immigrants stabilized. A number came as colonial administrators of all ranks and social origins, from aristocratic viceroys to modest bureaucrats looking for better salaries and promotions. Others came as idealistic missionaries. But most were humble commoners anxious to improve their lot as small entrepreneurs, skilled workers, or land-hungry peasants. They were encouraged to emigrate by letters from relatives and friends in the colonies telling them how abundant the food was, how good earnings were, and how many opportunities there were for a hard worker compared with the situation prevailing in Europe.

If the European immigration was important for its dynamic and elitist role, the African one was the most significant in numerical terms. While a few black slaves came from Spain with their masters in the very early days, slave trade from Africa started in about 1528 for the Spanish colonies and about 1550 for Brazil. Imports were small at first (some 500 slaves per year on the average), but in 1601–1650 Brazil received an average of 4,000 per year and the Spanish colonies 2,900. The estimated totals of black immigrants arriving in Latin America before 1650 are 250,000 for Brazil and 202,500 for Spanish America— almost half a million people. In both cases the peak of slave imports occurred in 1601–1625.

Slaves could be found in every colonial city (except the poorest and coldest ones) as domestic servants and artisans, though in small numbers. They were frequently able to buy their freedom or received it from their masters after long years of service. But most of the Africans went to rural or semirural areas in the tropical lowlands as replacements for the declining pool of Indian manpower in these depopulated territories. They cultivated export crops in Brazil and Venezuela, mined gold in western Colombia, and built fortifications and served as longshoremen in Panama, Cartagena, Veracruz, and many Caribbean ports. Toiling in large and growing gangs under overseers and without personal contact with their masters, their work was harder, their lives shorter, and their fate sadder than was the case for those in the cities.

Miscegenation was intense from the start, mainly because the immigrants were predominantly adult males. During the first half of the sixteenth century, ten males came from Castile for every female; the ratio for Portugal was even more unbalanced. The effective polygamy of many Iberians and their easy contact with Indian women soon produced a large number of half-breeds. In addition, white males and black females produced mulattoes, primarily in tropical areas. Later miscegenation between blacks and Indians gave rise to a third stock of half-breeds.

Coming from the racial melting pot of Iberia, Spaniards and Portuguese were not racially ethnocentric, but they were strongly prejudiced by their religion against the "infidel" or "heathen." So an Indian woman could be a perfect wife or mistress if she was baptized, and a mestizo son was considered a Spaniard or a Portuguese if he was legitimate. The strongest prejudice in sixteenth-century Latin America was directed against illegitimacy. It was even stronger in the case of mulattoes because it was compounded with disdain for the mother's slave condition or origin. So many biological half-breeds were considered white if they were legitimate and Spanish-educated, or Indian if they were illegitimate and raised among Indians. In 1570 blacks, mestizos, and mulattoes constituted only 2.5 percent of the total population in social terms, though in biological terms the percentage must have been considerably higher. In 1650, 12.7 percent of the total population was considered either black, mestizo, or mulatto. This percentage increase shows not only a biological trend but also the beginning of a certain degree of social discrimination against half-breeds. We will soon see why.

THE FAMILY    The European presence in the New World meant, in social terms, the transplantation of the Iberian family. While tolerance of other family structures was probably wider than is generally believed, the quick Hispanicization of the native aristocracies and gradual Christianization of the Indian masses were accompanied by widespread diffusion of the imported family structure.

The immigrants' sex ratio, though heavily unbalanced at the beginning in favor of males, was not sufficient to eradicate important family traits or to break social continuity with the Old World. But it was enough to attenuate the pattern of monogamy inherited from Europe. After years of sexual freedom the conquerors and early immigrants were too accustomed to easy sex and frequent polygamy to accept the theoretical role of faithful husbands. Their nostalgia for old times drew them together in friendships outside the domestic structure, and the relative abundance of slave and servant females created a durable pattern of extramarital sex life for males.

Therefore, when after several decades (sooner in Spanish America, later in Brazil) the sex ratio among Europeans had been balanced by female immigration, demographic growth, and assimilation of many mestizo females, the Spanish wife was generally unable to recapture her husband's former, and always reluctant, habit of marital fidelity. But since a long tradition of Muslim polygamy, courtly love, and male philandering in Europe had conditioned her to accept the colonial situation, she rarely complained about an unfaithful husband. She excelled as a mother and the core of the family but was not a passionate lover—though there were exceptions in both real life and literary myth. Marriage was a family alliance whose purpose was social promotion, not a personal matter of romance or love; romance was usually confined to innocent daydreaming or religious sublimation, while love was expressed in an intense maternal passion for one's children—and occasionally one's husband. What the legitimate wife never surrendered was her position as mother, effective head of the family, personnel manager and administrator of the household, and dignified matron. In addition, she played a major role as educator of the family, including husband and servants; this was the main cause of the persistent social religiosity of the Hispanic world. All this she accomplished with apparent submission to the patriarchal, externally respected husband, which meant an almost incredible .amount of feminine tact, patience, and diplomacy.

Iberians of both sexes had in common a strong feeling of lineage. An old Spanish family motto, worth quoting in its original formal beauty and childish arrogance, says *Antes que Dios fuera Dios/y los peñascos, peñascos,/los Quirós eran Quirós/y los Velascos, Velascos.* Or, in more pedestrian terms, the Quirós-Velasco family proclaimed to believe itself older (and nobler by implication) than the oldest rocks and even God. This feeling accounted for a tight-knit family structure with lasting effects. Among these was a relatively late coming of age (at the twenty-fifth birthday) and durable dependence on and respect for the parents.

The sense of lineage also generated a strong desire for children as proof of the husband's virility, the wife's fertility, and the blessing of God, as well as to perpetuate the family name and perhaps enhance it. One result was the tendency to create a *mayorazgo*, or entail to perpetuate through the eldest son the family's patrimony; this went as far as wealth and legal controls permitted. The younger brothers and sisters were cared for and assisted by the eldest, who was the head of the family after the father's death. Another effect of family pride was a father's more than usual care for the future and education of his illegitimate offspring, an attitude tacitly tolerated by his legitimate wife.

A further effect was the crucial role of relatives: If they were rich, they were expected to help; if influential, they must offer recommendations, jobs, and useful introductions;

if poor, they might be offered a place in the household, employment in the family business, or at least maintenance as loyal and reliable quasiservants. Finally, family pride was symbolized (according to the traditions of the Mediterranean world) by the most fragile treasure of the "weakest" half of the family: female premarital virginity and marital fidelity. Easy interracial sex and attenuated monogamy on the part of the white males made possible this cult of family honor with only limited recourse to full-time professional female prostitution, which in the colonies never reached the massive proportions prevalent in the Mediterranean world.

Beyond the coercive but protective sphere of the extended family the Iberian colonist was reluctant to go. Friendship and religion were the only solid links with an outside world that was by definition cold, distant, and hostile, where only God and king existed as distant symbols of hope and justice. The only reliable social unit beyond the family was the Iberian village or town from which a colonist had emigrated, where everybody knew everybody else and both friendships and hatreds endured for generations. A paisano (a man from the same hometown) or a friend was the next best thing to the family. Partners, confidants, and associates were always chosen from among relatives and paisanos—loyalty and reliability were preferred over competence, efficiency, and intelligence. Open nepotism was not considered an abuse but was a universal practice with logical foundations. (This, by the way, explains many historical characteristics of the Hispanic world, from the late advent of chartered companies and impersonal business corporations to personal, charismatic political leadership: The corporation does not inspire confidence, and has no face to slap or to kiss, and the same goes for a Constitution or a faceless political party.)

Thus the town of origin gradually became an idealized memory that eventually, after several generations, was replaced by a stronger and livelier attachment to the new home town in Latin America. If a turning point can be established in this slow process, it would be the early seventeenth century, when the American-born Spaniards proudly started to call themselves criollos (creoles) and invented pejorative terms for new immigrants. All this helps explain in psychological terms both the durability of the colonial regime and the inevitability of its end.

Good friends were almost equivalent to members of the family. They said of themselves, "we love each other as brothers (or sisters)," friendship being a one-sex business for the sake of compatibility with the above-mentioned symbols of family honor ("Man is fire, woman is tow, the devil comes and blows," as the old Spanish proverb goes). On another level, servants and employees of long standing were also considered part of the family. Friends and servants both contributed to the prestige of the family as valuable connections or status symbols, respectively. This gift of social prestige was paid for (in the case of servants) with protection and care for life and (in the case of friends) with one of the most gracious forms of hospitality that civilization has invented. The occasional visitor with good credentials and even the jester and the parasite were tolerated, if not welcomed, because—as another family motto has it—"to give is lordly, to receive is servile." Hospitality, full of nuances but always generous, contributed in some way to the social luster of the family.

The family increased in size and importance through religious kinship. A child's godparents assumed the spiritual relationship and social duties defined by Church tradition and law, but the system also served the wider purposes of strengthening friendships, obtaining protection and help from a rich or powerful connection, or dispensing such help or protection to needy clients. A less intimate but broader form of religious kinship existed through lay religious associations or sodalities, technically functional units of cult and spiritual life within a parish but socially serving as exclusive multipurpose clubs whose functions included mutual aid, welfare, and charity programs. These associations or brotherhoods were adopted by Christianized Indians from the 1570s on; in the seventeenth century they were widely diffused and gave Indian communities a ritual life, a ceremonial expression, and a prestige system (for the stewards of the sodalities) that they badly needed. Guilds and other professional associations also had a religious dimension in the cults of their patron saints, and many offered the privileges of mutual benefit associations. Such professional bodies resembled peculiar and limited family forms, with a smaller component of love and a larger one of hatred and formal dependence. The "colleague" did not exist: He was either a personal and loyal friend, a distant competitor, or a bitter enemy.

The "lone wolf" had no place in Hispanic society. Even a bachelor or a secular priest was the head of a family consisting of his widowed mother, unmarried sisters, or other relatives and servants (as many as income allowed). The sexual urges of these patriarchs were discreetly satisfied outside the home. A bachelor was often able to provide for an undemanding mistress but did not have the economic means to support a wife in addition to his widowed mother and unmarried sisters; finding husbands for them had priority over getting a wife for himself. A man living alone was a social outcast. In urban areas he was a resident guest in his landlady's house or an apprentice or servant in his employer's home. In rural environments the loner was either a farmhand (the counterpart of the urban apprentice or servant), a runaway slave, or a totally destitute vagrant of any race. The slave tried to reach some remote community of fellow deserters; the vagrants sometimes joined forces to make a living through rural banditry. In both cases they kidnapped women and took them to their hideouts. But the dangers of cruel repression inclined most nonblack vagrants to go to the big cities and somehow integrate themselves into the growing ranks of beggars and habitual delinquents or the lowest proletarian levels, where total and undiscriminating racial miscegenation was practiced. Persistent loners were familiar with deportations, fights, jails, hospitals, and the alms of meals at the door of some convent.

Life in monasteries and convents also had a family dimension: Each religious community was by definition a spiritual family, though its internal quarrels (sometimes of violent city-wide impact) usually had very worldly manifestations in spite of their supposedly spiritual origins. Monks usually did parish duty, and through this and the confessional—where they and the secular priests acted as family counselors, psychiatrists, and psychoanalysts—they exercised great social influence. The convent churches or chapels, together with the ordinary church parishes, were the main centers for community gatherings, and their locutories and sacristies frequently served as men's clubs in the monasteries and women's clubs in the convents. Lay religious associations of many kinds and the church-operated elementary schools served as much-used social bridges between the religious communities and the rest of the city.

In spite of the number and size of the convents, however, married life was the dominant pattern, even more than in the parent country. The status of housewife was every woman's ideal and was enjoyed (more or less) by at least nine out of ten. In contrast with the small number of foreigners among male immigrants, all the women of European origin were Iberian or deeply Iberianized before immigration. Respectable widows with grown-up children and married women who had to make a living worked as midwives, healers, bakers, confectioners, dressmakers, seamstresses or landladies—the only professions besides domestic service and prostitution that were open to women. Wealthier women usually invested their dowries and personal money in real estate, slaves (for domestic service and profitable rental), or money-lending; any other form of investment was considered suitable for men only. A spinster or a childless widow, if she was unable to remarry soon, had only four honorable options: to live with her parents, to act as housekeeper for a bachelor brother, to live with a married sister and help her with child care, or to go to a convent. This explains the large number of convents and their apparent lack of discipline—most convents were not only centers of religious life but also dignified refuges for lonely women as nuns or as lay residents. Their cells were consequently of two different types: Some were small, ascetic corners where mystic souls waited for their eternal marriage with Christ; others were rich apartments with several rooms and a team of female servants and slaves, where a woman could afford to live by herself with a tolerable degree of external control.

In summary, the extended family was, in one form or another, the core of social organization. As such, each one established alliances with other families to form social constellations whose size and profile were carefully planned. New alliances were made through marriage, which at high social levels played a parallel role to that of royal marriages in international policy. As each family included several social strata, from the patrons at the top to the clients at the bottom, feuds between families and constellations of families created the social conflicts and tensions often mistaken for political problems. Patriarchalism and social paternalism developed freely until the middle of the eighteenth century; their very gradual decline began later, when traditional family loyalties were transferred to other social, economic, and political institutions.

URBAN SOCIETIES Most Spanish colonial cities were built on formerly uninhabited sites. When a new city was established on the site of an Indian one, the latter was leveled or drastically remodeled because its urban structures and functions were too different from those of Spanish cities. In any case, though the building task was immense for both early settlers and Indian workers, the circumstances made possible an extremely modern type of city planning. Colonial cities could develop without the usual constraints found in Europe: encircling medieval walls, irregular layout, narrow and winding streets, high real-estate prices. In America, with plenty of free land and manpower, cities were built according to the latest architectural concepts of the European Renaissance. Both amateur and professional architects, engineers, and constructors seized the opportunity and frequently did a good job of it. Local differences in topography, climate, building materials, and landscape saved these new cities from the monotony and uniformity that could have resulted from the fact that most of them were built within a short span of time and, therefore, under the same aesthetic and technical principles. Some mistakes were made, and the locations of a number of cities were changed in order to remedy such errors. In general, however, climatic and sanitary factors were taken into consideration before construction began, in addition to the availability of water, fertile land, wood, and building materials.

The Spanish-American city was planned around a central square where the town hall, the main church or the cathedral, and public offices were built. Around this plaza two sets of parallel streets crossing each other perpendicularly determined rectangular or square blocks, in which each resident was given a lot. The larger the lot and the closer it was to the plaza, the greater the prestige and prominence of the recipient. Many lots remained vacant to be given to latecomers. These were granted free and with full ownership rights if the beneficiary built his house and remained for a given length of time as a resident; later he was free to sell the lot and house without restriction.

Initially a typical city consisted of a number of scattered family shelters (mainly simple huts) surrounded by improvised vegetable gardens. But the growth of the city pushed up the market value of the soil until the houses were close together; interior gardens became a rare luxury. The typical Spanish house of southern Castile, derived from the ancient Roman house with its sober and massive façade, its central yard with rooms around it, and its backyard and stable (the garage of those days), was transplanted to this continent. As much money and effort as possible were invested in making the house a showcase suited to the prestige of its owner and his family.

In due course a few streets became commercial ones as artisans of several trades chose to live in the same neighborhood, selling their products at the entrances of their homes. Shops and pubs soon proliferated along these streets. The central square became a large community concourse that was always active—as a marketplace in the mornings and a social gathering place in the late afternoons (the best place for a leisurely stroll—a pleasure unknown to other civilizations—conversation, girl watching, and gossip). It was also the setting for solemnities of all kinds: religious processions, public receptions for political and religious authorities, civic celebrations, bullfights, sports, and executions of convicted criminals. The best and most expensive houses were always close to the plaza.

The area reserved for urban building was never less than 600 yards square and usually much larger than that; its profile was quite regular if there were no natural obstacles. Steep hills, rivers, main roads, and coastlines modified the urban perimeter, which was often embellished along such natural features with tree-shaded public walks, which competed with the central square during the hot summers as social centers and were later transformed into beautiful boulevards or city parks. In the suburbs the Indian districts appeared early, forming satellite urban neighborhoods sometimes separated from the downtown area but always functionally connected to the rest of the city.

The physical plan of the Brazilian city was similar to the Spanish one but more modest in appearance and size, and comparatively irregular in layout. Most of the early Brazilian cities were agrocommercial ports along the coast that followed the Portuguese model of city-ports.

Beyond the urban perimeter the city had at least several square leagues of territory, which was its patrimony. Part of this area was designated for free use by all the residents for slaughterhouses and threshing floors, grazing fields (only for the few pigs, goats, pets, and heads of cattle that each resident reared at home for meat, milk, fun, and transportation, respectively), free supply of firewood, and controlled use of timber. The rest of the territory remained unused unless an Indian community was living there, in which case the Indian lands were supposed to be respected by the white settlers. Tracts of this vacant land were given to residents for cultivation, upon request, on the same terms as those governing urban lots. The standard grants were a *peonía* (given to a peon, or foot soldier, after the conquest) or a *caballería* (given to a cavalry man). The former was variable in size, depending on climate and soil quality, but large enough to provide subsistence for the average family; the latter was roughly twice the size of the former.

These grants were the origin of the first farms, operated by city dwellers, eventually with Spanish employees and Indian farm hands; the latter were obtained through either encomienda or any other system of forced labor. Grazing permits were also granted to urban residents so that they could raise herds of cattle, pigs, sheep, and goats on the vacant land. The beneficiaries managed sooner or later to obtain formal or de facto ownership of these grazing lands, thus establishing the first commercial livestock ranches. These farms and ranches, fully devoted to European agriculture and livestock production, were the scene of the first stage of the American economic revolution, in which European crops, livestock, and agricultural and cattle-raising technology were introduced.

The whole system had two main causes. The first was economic, representing an effort to supply the cities with traditional European foodstuffs. (The Indians could not be taught overnight to be good farmers and shepherds using new techniques, animals, and seeds.) The second was the lust for land ownership on the part of the many landless peasants among the Spanish immigrants. A contributing factor was the traditional Castilian ideal of the landlord as the epitome of wealth, respectability, and social prestige. In Portuguese Brazil a parallel trend appeared, but from the earliest days it favored the big landlords and the seignorial way of life associated with ownership of large sugar plantations.

The spontaneous early system of land grants sketched here—accepted by the Castilian Crown in the Ordinances of 1573—eventually used up the city's territory. As the hunger for land grew instead of decreasing, the cities tried to extend their territorial jurisdiction through negotiation with other cities, concession of new lands by the king, or illegal appropriation of Indian lands. As we will see, the Crown tried to solve the problem with an agrarian reform in 1591.

The city was ruled, policed, and administered by an institution of medieval origin and profile: the Castilian *cabildo* (equivalent, with minor variations, to the *senado da camara* in Portugal and its colonies). The *cabildo* was a council, in theory elected by all the resident family heads but in practice more or less oligarchic, consisting of two to six aldermen or councillors, two justices of the peace, a market inspector, and a standard-bearer. Several paid employees did the technical and paper work; these included an occasional municipal attorney, a city clerk, a jailer, a doorkeeper, and others. The size of the council depended on the wealth and importance of the city. Its vitality and effectiveness was considerable in the early days. As soon as most of the city land had been granted to individuals, the power of the municipal council began to decrease because it had less and less to give. (No local taxes were levied, the only municipal income being rents from the patrimony and small custom fees on some items brought into the city.) However, the council's duties increased as the city grew; it continued to serve as general administrator, financer, and manager of public works; keeper of the town hall, the jail, and other public buildings; local administrator of justice; custodian of law and order in the streets; inspector of markets, weights, and measures; and manager of a myriad of other minor but vital community services.

In early times there were candidates in every election for municipal jobs because everybody was eager to acquire status, prestige, and a part in the granting of land. When the greediest and most influential citizens had achieved these goals, "civic spirit" started to vanish and each man would rather worry about his own generally prosperous business than toil in the council for the benefit of the community. This was the central reason for the decline of the municipal councils, though it is customary to attribute their demise to the growing importance of royal officers and the monopoly of aldermen's jobs by a small, self-perpetuating, oligarchic group. In Brazil this did not happen until the eighteenth century; the *senado da camara* remained active, and in it the local guilds were represented by a people's tribune.

In Spanish America the *cabildo* was at first monopolized by the *encomenderos,* but the decline of this elite opened the council to lawyers, non-*encomendero* landowners, merchants, and others. The oligarchy in control of municipal power varied from one city to another, depending on the relative strength of local pressure groups. However, the decline of the *cabildo* has probably been overemphasized. In Mexico City and Lima, where the viceroy was evidently the local boss, the *cabildo* found in him, at least, an attentive ear, while in small cities the councillors, as a local elite, carried more weight—even if only because of their permanence—than the resident officer of the Crown—a temporary appointee—even though he presided over their sessions. Low attendance at meetings and seemingly sterile precedence disputes during the seventeenth century did not mean lack of administrative work (carried out by the *cabildo's* employees), loss of political punch, or institutional paralysis. Occasional local protests, scandals, and even riots were proof of strong political undercurrents and a thrust of majority public opinion. Because all was usually quiet in the city, one should not envision a cataleptic city life under dead municipal institutions, but rather business as usual and things under control.

In the first chapter we sketched the early social profile of the colonial city. After the conquest period the social body grew in both size and complexity, and experienced dynamic changes—though it did not undergo any structural revolution. The initial oligarchy of *encomenderos* declined and partly vanished, but in part it transformed into a new elite of rich landowners, gradually enlarged by others who had never been *encomenderos.* These rich landowners (*hacendados* in Spanish America, *senhores de engenhos* in Brazil) had their wealth in rural property, but their official residences and social power in the cities; thus they formed local aristocracies. Their prestige was based on the Iberian tradition of big land ownership as a noble way of life; their power resided in their control of people (employees and farm hands) and resources (land, commercial crops, and livestock with solid market value). Their main privilege consisted in the cumulative equity they enjoyed as owners of progressively more valuable real estate, and their solidarity as a pressure group permitted them to obtain the lowest tax rates in the colonies. Finally, their perpetuation as a dominant group was accomplished through *mayorazgo*, which avoided the partition of their holdings, and marriage alliances, which enlarged and consolidated their properties.

On the other hand the concentration of overseas trade and the resultant monopolistic and oligopolistic practices (see chapter 2) gave rise to powerful groups of *mercaderes*, or wholesale merchants. Their power resided in their capital in cash, which made them not only monopolistic traders but also financial magnates as short-term money lenders (and practically bankers) for the rest of the social body. They even financed the state through tolerably high taxes, profitable "donations" in cash, advances of money, and subscription of government and war loans. They were initially subject to suspicion and the prejudice traditionally held toward their profession, but they rapidly acquired prestige owing to their wealth in an increasingly materialistic society. The founding of their powerful guilds in Mexico City (1592) and Lima (1613) consolidated their social respectability and gave them an instrument for institutional self-perpetuation as an effective pressure group. In addition, the most prominent landowners and merchants were able to top off their economic preeminence during the seventeenth century by buying titles of nobility from bankrupt kings willing to sell almost anything for cash. Thus these potentates succeeded where the conquerors had failed.

Marriage alliances connected both dominant elites, whose power pervaded the whole society through their clients. In many regions the *hacendados* represented the interests of lesser landowners, whom they could control, intimidate, or destroy at will. The *mercaderes* controlled lesser merchants, down to the poorest shopkeepers and peddlers, as well as the humblest artisans, through their credits and supplies; we have seen how they controlled the miners too. In the tradition of a corporate society, this system of patrons and clients easily took hold, making impossible for centuries the formation of true social classes (and much more class consciousness) even in an increasingly capitalistic world. If the *hacendados* had a good year, some of the benefits reached not only lesser landowners but also employees and farm hands. Since the same can be said about bad years, the boom-bust alternative represented for the landless peasant either work (with low pay) or unemployment and famine. In a parallel way profitable business or lack of it filtered down to the smallest fish in the commercial profession. As a result common interests developed "vertically" (from top to bottom of society) by economic sector rather than "horizontally" by social class as in modern industrial societies. The resulting sectoral development of loyalties and common interest gave to colonial society its enduring traditionalism, strength, and relative stability.

The middle groups of bureaucrats, employees, professional men, and secular priests that started to appear in the cities after the conquest grew later as a result of more openings in the expanding ranks of the clergy and the public administration; moreover, there was increasing demand for their services in the ever-larger and more sophisticated cities. These salaried white-collar professionals, the core of a potential middle class, were recruited among relatively educated European immigrants and graduates of the colleges and universities established early in the colonial period. As the job market became more competitive because of the high social prestige attached to nonmanual work, the bitter competition for jobs began to have important social consequences: antagonism between European-born and criollo Spaniards, and the development of prejudice against educated mestizos. Qualified criollos resented the competitive presence of those whom they considered "outsiders" in the job market. Their professional jealousy and envy soon took the form of prejudice against immigrants and half-breeds. In addition, the social stigma attached to illegitimacy was unduly generalized and used as a weapon against mestizo competitors. The short-term result of this criollo attitude was professional discrimination against mestizos in a number of religious and public positions; in the long term it would expand to the rest of the social body, generating a strong social (if not racial) prejudice and consolidating in the eighteenth century a caste society with explosive potential. Many scions of elite families deprived by *mayorazgo* of succession to their family patrimonies, received an education that qualified them (with help from their elders) for membership in the middle groups. These criollo professionals had considerable success in closing the ranks of the middle groups to qualified immigrants and mestizos, thanks mainly to the nepotistic pressure applied by their families but also to the growing discrimination against those two groups. The predominance of criollos of elite social origin (reversed during the eighteenth century at great political risk) accounted for the subservient attitude of the middle groups toward the colonial social elites. Hence, one of the later traits differentiating Latin American from European societies was the lack of a large, socially independent, politically self-conscious, early consolidated, and intellectually creative and self-centered middle class.

Two important social elites, the high clergy and the colonial officers, will be dealt with in the next chapter. It will suffice here to say that they operated under the same principles that affected the others. Each urban society was original and unique in its way of integrating the several social sectors and groups. Even if the constituent elements were the same, their relative importance and size in a city's social structure had almost infinite variations. The agricultural cities were controlled mainly by the social elite of landowners; the commercial ones, by the merchant elite as the most powerful pressure group. The mining cities were the only ones in which the rich miners had an important role, while in cities where livestock was the main commercial product, local elites of cattle barons emerged. Entrepreneurs prospered in industrial cities, having a hand in city life, and the symbiotic association of clergy and royal bureaucracy predominated in cities that had been chosen as headquarters of religious and political power.

RURAL
COMMUNITIES
Until about 1550 the Indians of Brazil remained almost undisturbed by Europeans. Meanwhile in Spanish America the conquerors destroyed the Indian ruling elites and built new cities, leaving the rural areas to the Indians. Economic, political, and cultural intercourse between Europeans and Indians began immediately on a limited scale. The cities attracted both human and economic resources from the rural areas; a small but growing number of Indians settled in the cities and their surrounding estancias, and were quickly Hispanicized and integrated into the colonial society. Nevertheless, most of the natives preferred to remain in their own communities, and for a while the encomienda was the only bridge between the cities and the rural Indian settlements.

The early *encomenderos* were urban dwellers, visiting the countryside only on sporadic inspection trips. They were not prepared to deal directly with the Indians and therefore respected the integrity of the native communities and the authority of the local leaders who served as intermediaries between the mass of vassals and the new Castilian lords. Called caciques in Mesoamerica and *curacas* in Peru, the Indian chieftains were either confirmed in their jobs or replaced by more docile individuals but were in any case perpetuated under Spanish inheritance laws as a lesser rural nobility. Through them the *encomenderos* exercised a sort of indirect rule over the Indians, trying to maximize the amount of forced labor and tribute they received from the caciques but leaving to them the task of exacting it and presiding over the Indians' traditional economic and social structures. In due course the *encomenderos* were gradually eliminated as an elite of feudal lords, and the function of the encomienda changed: it ceased to be a seignorial institution implying rule over the natives and became merely the right of the *encomendero* to receive a certain amount of money in cash out of the tribute collected from the Indians. When the tribute payments were regulated by the Crown so as not to exceed the amounts paid by the Indians to their lords before the arrival of the Europeans, encomienda was transformed into a rent and, progressively taxed and reduced, lost its former importance.

Between the 1530s and the 1550s, a new system of native administration was initiated that later spread to all of the Spanish colonies. It consisted of public officers appointed to the royal bureaucracy for two or three years as *corregidores de indios*. Assisted by a number of deputies, subaltern employees, and interpreters, they presided over the Indian caciques and *curacas*. The *corregidor de indios* was paid a salary and made responsible for ruling a rural district, administering justice in the king's name, collecting tribute from the head of each Indian community, and allocating the forced Indian labor indispensable to the Spanish cities, mines, and estancias. Although the purpose of the new system was to moderate the demands on Indian tribute and labor, abuses were rampant. Many *corregidores de indios* pressed the caciques to deliver more and more tribute and manpower, the latter far above the percentage established by law (a maximum of 4 percent of the native population in New Spain, 7 percent in Peru). In order to satisfy Indian complaints, a summary court of justice for Indian affairs was established in New Spain; elsewhere magistrates were appointed for the same purpose. The flow of complaints to the court and magistrates was very large, but their effectiveness was limited. However, though abuses and corruption eventually existed at all levels of the native administration, it is only fair to note that, especially after the 1550s, the pressure on the *corregidores de indios* increased considerably. The compound impact of demographic and economic factors imposed a heavier demand on a shrinking manpower pool: The economic takeoff stimulated by the discovery of the silver mines plus the subsequent growth of the cities required more and more manpower, just when the accumulated impact of high mortality due to epidemics had left less Indian manpower available than ever.

In the 1570s the situation became critical. Many Indian communities had disappeared as a result of depopulation and compulsory labor; the Indians either fled to remote areas to avoid forced work and tribute payments or settled in the Spanish cities where, as Hispanicized proletarians, they seem to have been exploited less. Excessive allocation of manpower to the mines, wasteful use of human resources in city building, and growing depopulation combined to produce a decline in agricultural output. Public administrators at all levels complained about the lack of unskilled labor and even feared that the Indians would become totally extinct. The cities complained of higher food prices and occasional food shortages; they did their best to control prices and regulate markets, but to no avail. The growing cost and scarcity of agricultural produce motivated a search for long-term solutions that gave rise to two important developments: the regrouping of rural Indians in new villages and the beginning of large-scale European agriculture. Both points deserve elaboration because of their far-reaching consequences.

In order to Christianize the Indians, the early missionaries had invented the trick of attracting them to the missions as permanent settlers. Between the 1570s and the early 1600s, the colonial administration followed this model on a large scale, but with some changes and for different purposes. In an attempt to save the Indians from extinction and to increase agricultural production, laymen instead of friars were commissioned to establish new Indian villages as viable peasant communities; vagrant Indians, decimated former settlements, and other small clusters of Indians were regrouped and concentrated in new, relatively large villages. The new groups were given lands (free, in perpetuity, and unalienable) and settled in *pueblos de indios,* or Indian villages, that were predominantly European in structure but under Indian rule. Some natives went happily to the *pueblos* and others were persuaded to resettle, but most were forced to move, under the leadership of an Indian cacique and the supervision of a *corregidor de indios*.

The new Indian villages were a balanced mixture of aboriginal and European elements. Their physical plan was a replica of the Castilian small town, though simpler and poorer. The land was owned, in the local tradition, not by individuals but by the community. One-third was for cultivation, one-third for pastures, and the rest for commercial production. The cash flow from the commercial production was used to meet the community's needs in terms of capitalization, tools and livestock, savings, and the like. Non-Indians were forbidden to settle in the *pueblo's* territory or even to stop there as travelers for more than a couple of days; this was to protect the community from disruptive encroachments.

The operation of the system varied from place to place, and results ranged from full success to total failure. The cacique acted sometimes as a responsible community leader and sometimes as a rascal; the same can be said about the supervising *corregidor de indios* and the parish priest appointed for each *pueblo*. In general, however, community life took hold quickly. The Indians were basically Christianized in a few generations, but it was only a matter of years before they became familiar with European seeds, animals, and agricultural and cattle-raising techniques; a peculiar version of the municipal *cabildo* was developed; and the sale of their commercial crops integrated these communities into the European capitalistic economy and long-distance trade, gradually expanding their limited potential as consumers. In contrast with the Indians who settled in cities and were culturally assimilated and totally Hispanicized, these communities were cultural melting pots of native and European elements that created lasting mestizo cultures. Their originality expressed itself in their clothing, folk art, rural architecture, and folk music, sometimes reaching high aesthetic levels. They also developed their own religiosity, a syncretic mixture of Catholicism and innumerable purely aboriginal ritual observances and superstitions. Finally, in spite of the benevolent paternalism pervading the whole system, many communities soon acquired enough knowledge of the colonial machinery and enough feeling for the community's interests to fight in the courts for their lands and rights against corrupt administrators and land-hungry Spaniards and mestizos. The survival of many *pueblos de indios* until Independence proves that they were generally successful in preserving their municipal institutions and their lands.

The second point to summarize is the beginning of large-scale European agriculture. We saw the early settlers receiving free land within the cities. Since the early urban settlements were small, relatively isolated, and self-sufficient, their needs were limited; in consequence, a pattern of small or medium-sized land ownership emerged. Crops and livestock were raised in the early family gardens and on farms under Spanish supervision. They used a small manpower force consisting of slaves brought from overseas and alienated Indians who chose to settle with the Spaniards, worked for wages, and were soon Hispanicized. These permanent, skilled farm hands were temporarily supplemented by unskilled Indian forced labor, through encomienda in the early days and later through a system of allocations administered by the *corregidores de indios*. As the cities grew and the mines created a heavy manpower demand, and at the same time the number of Indians decreased, the unavoidable result was a crisis in agricultural production. This challenge was met by Spanish entrepreneurs with quick development of European crop and livestock production, stimulated by growing demand and higher prices. Legal or illegal appropriation of land vacated by Indian communities or never before cultivated must have reached vast proportions.

A royal decree issued in 1591 proclaimed that all vacant lands except the territory of each city, existing land grants, and lands actually cultivated by Indian communities were public domains and would be granted from then on via public auctions, with the proceeds going to the royal treasury. This decree proved, among other things, that the era of free grants was over: Land already had market value and was in strong demand. On the other hand the first stockmen's association in the New World, created on the Castilian model, had been approved by the king in 1542. Thus commercial agriculture and livestock production, fully capitalistic in character, soared during the second half of the sixteenth century.

The early pattern of small and medium-sized landholdings persisted in a few areas, but in many regions this pattern evolved toward the consolidation of larger and larger estates. There were several reasons for this. Land was the least risky form of investment, and the taxes on land were the lowest and the last to be enforced. The growth of the cities provided an expanding and profitable market for crops and livestock, which in turn made land the capital growth investment *par excellence*. Moreover, the landlord remained an ideal of social prestige, dignity, and economic stability for the Iberians; a large estate was always entailed in order to prevent its division and ensure its remaining in the family. Marriage alliances and investment of commercial and mining profits also contributed to mergers and consolidation of landholdings. This was the origin of the seventeenth-century Spanish hacienda.

The hacienda can be defined as a very large, rural, entailed estate in a temperate region, owned by an individual (*hacendado*). It was simultaneously an economic enterprise and a well-defined rural community or microsociety. Its production was diversified and it was almost self-sufficient, but it always raised commercial crops destined for the colonial domestic sector. Some haciendas were devoted mainly to agriculture, others to raising livestock.

From the social standpoint the hacienda was a patriarchal society presided over by the owner with his family and retinue of employees (stewards, foremen, artisans), dependants, and servants. A chaplain, frequently a relative of the master, took care of the chapel, the community's religious life, and the schooling of the children. A small permanent staff of farm hands and cowboys (free workers, mainly mestizos and Indians, receiving either payment in kind or money wages and the right to cultivate small plots for themselves and their families) was supplemented during busy seasons by temporary workers from Indian communities and neighboring towns; those workers were paid money wages.

The master had his residence on the hacienda but kept a house in the city and traveled back and forth for business and social reasons. His lordly way of life, his paternalistic rule over employees and workers, his economic self-sufficiency and relative seclusion, and the similarity between his retinue and that of the early *encomendero* have inclined many historians to refer to the "feudal" character of the hacienda. Granted that, from a social perspective, the *hacendado* tended to act in his domain not only as owner but also as lord, judge, and even god, this had more to do with the structure of the extended family than with any survival of feudalism.

In economic terms the hacienda was fully capitalistic: It could not survive without selling commercial crops or cattle to the city market. Its self-sufficiency, usually interpreted as a trait of a precapitalistic economy, was in reality sensible economic diversification in the orthodox capitalist style. Its low rentability and its vast size, with only part of the soil under cultivation—a cardinal sin for worshipers of economic development and full-capacity production—were the outgrowths of the shrewd capitalistic policy of producing just as much as the market could absorb at good prices. (Moreover, idle land was productive in terms of equity because land prices were always rising.) Finally, the *hacendado's* typical land hunger, leading him to continually enlarge his property through marriage, purchase, or usurpation, was not a form of megalomania but had the truly capitalistic motive of acquiring as much land as possible in order to reduce the competition in the city market. A close counterpart of the Spanish hacienda, the Brazilian fazenda developed during the seventeenth century.

Let us now compare the haciendas and fazendas to the *engenhos* and *ingenios azucareros* described earlier. The main difference was that the *engenhos* were located in tropical climates and the haciendas in temperate zones. Moreover, the *engenhos*, with more abundant capital and greater marketing opportunities, found it advantageous to specialize in their most profitable crop to the point of monoculture, while the haciendas, with less capital and smaller and less profitable markets, wisely diversified their production. Finally, the *engenhos*, located in areas where unskilled manpower was scarce, found it rewarding to import expensive slaves from overseas, while the haciendas, unable to buy slaves in quantity, had to manage with local manpower at low wages or compulsory Indian labor. Thus differences in environment, climate, markets, available resources, and business opportunities suffice to explain all of the structural differences between haciendas and fazendas on the one side and *ingenios* and *engenhos* on the other. Both types of estate were actually variations of the same model.

If a general trend was discernible in rural areas, it was the gradual shrinking of the Indian population, culture, and closed precapitalistic economy. On the other hand there was a gradual expansion, beginning in the second half of the sixteenth century, of European capitalistic agriculture, oriented toward the cities and open to long-distance trade. If this process had followed its spontaneous course, the predictable result would have been the vanishing of the Indian population through total assimilation into the new European stock; the surviving elements of Indian culture would have been integrated into the Iberian colonial variant of Western civilization. But a complex mixture of fiscal, economic, and ethical reasons moved the Crown to design—and colonial society to accept—a policy that limited this trend and complicated its historical consequences. The creation of *pueblos de indios* gave the Indian stock a chance to survive the deadly impact of European epidemics and to recover demographically over time; Indian cultural traditions survived in the *pueblos*, and a mestizo colonial culture had time to develop. The Indian world, though decimated and altered, was thus able to survive. The process was not uniform, however. In areas where European immigrants settled in dense clusters around large cities, the Indian world disappeared completely. But in rural zones and small provincial towns where Europeans settled in small numbers and the *pueblos de indios* took hold, Indian communities were thriving at the end of the colonial era, controlling in some cases over half the land under cultivation.

# Chapter 4

# The Quest for Utopia

M ost of the Iberian immigrants crossed the Atlantic in search of economic gain and social promotion. They created, as we have seen, a predominantly materialistic society in a framework of commercial capitalism. Nevertheless, two small groups went to the colonies with very different purposes: They were the friars, who supposedly emigrated for strictly religious reasons, and the officers of the king, who went overseas as professional bureaucrats to enforce the monarch's authority. In due time both groups formed social sectors which reached from the top strata of society (archbishops, viceroys) to the bottom (curates in poor Indian villages, modest soldiers, and local officers). The purpose of this chapter is to present some basic information about both groups and to evaluate their role in the colonies.

A NEW CHRISTENDOM    The first thing to remark is the social prestige enjoyed by these two groups. Respect for them was deeply rooted in Iberian medieval tradition. Priests, as ministers of God, were the depositaries of spiritual power, and royal officers exercised by delegation the undisputed political power of the king. Both groups were the visible colonial representa-

tives of the two universal symbols of hope and justice—
God and king. This was one reason for their vast social
influence, in spite of their small size; the other was their
stable alliance and symbiotic relationship, which mutually
enhanced their power and prestige. In the medieval tradition of Christian states, the kings of Castile and Portugal
had a duty to defend and protect the Church as well as
to foster an environment conducive to the eternal salvation of all of their subjects. The Church, for its part, had
a practical monopoly over education and public welfare,
performing a number of social functions that the state
would assume only in later times.

This traditional overlapping of responsibilities was
strongly reinforced by several papal bulls after 1493; the
most important of these was the *Universalis Ecclesiae*
(1508). Through such bulls the Pope granted in perpetuity
to the rulers of Castile the authority to establish and
organize churches overseas, to present candidates for all
of the sees and most clerical jobs, and to exact and spend
tithes. In 1514 the *Praecelsae devotionis* extended similar
privileges to the king of Portugal in his colonies. These
were the beginnings of an unprecedented situation in which
the Pope, unable to organize and finance the propagation of
the faith in the New World,* transferred this task to the
Spanish and Portuguese kings. They thus were granted
immense authority over the clergy of both empires as the
Pope's vicars in ecclesiastical administration and as patrons
of the Church in the colonies; the resulting system was
called *Patronato* in Spanish America, *Padroado* in Brazil.

In Europe the late Middle Ages had witnessed widespread attempts at religious renewal and the restoration of
a pure Christian life, unencumbered by medieval ceremony and tradition, and based on Christ's preaching and
the practices of his early followers. This trend was very
strong among the mendicant orders of friars during the

---

* A Sacred College of *Propaganda Fide* in charge of the missions
was not established in the Vatican until 1622, becoming effective
many years later.

late fifteenth century in Castile. Groups of strict observants developed a new austerity, a severe self-discipline, and a strong feeling of evangelical mission; among them it was easy to find the most suitable personnel—generous, idealistic, enthusiastic perfectionists—for the evangelization of the New World. The papal bull *Omnimoda* (1522) accordingly allowed them to undertake the sacramental and pastoral jobs normally entrusted to parish priests. But they had been active for many years before the *Omnimoda* was issued. In 1511, for example, the Dominican friar Antonio de Montesinos had denounced the settlers of Hispaniola to their faces in a courageous and virulent sermon:

. . . you are in mortal sin . . . for the cruelty and tyranny you use in dealing with these innocent people. . . . Tell me, by what right do you keep these Indians in such a cruel and horrible servitude? On what authority have you waged a detestable war against these people, who dwelt quietly and peacefully on their own land? . . . Are these not men? Have they not rational souls? Are you not bound [as Christians] to love them as you love yourselves?*

This sermon was just the beginning of a spirited defense of the rights of the Indians based on the Christian assumption that all men are brothers, equal before God. The Dominican friars were the most vocal combatants in a struggle for justice that lasted until the late sixteenth century and was carried out by jurists and theologians in many debates and advisory committees summoned by the king, as well as in the classrooms of Spanish universities. Bartolomé de Las Casas was the most outstanding activist, the most passionate defender of the Indians, and the moving force behind a number of protective laws enacted by the king that would have been admirable if they had been

---

* The substance of this sermon was preserved by Las Casas in *Historia de las Indias,* lib. 3, cap. 4, whence this quotation comes. The translation is Lewis Hanke's.

fully enforced in the colonies. Francisco de Vitoria, in his 1539 lectures at the University of Salamanca, showed that he was the most lucid intellectual analyzing the main philosophical and political issues raised by the Spanish colonization; he deserves to be counted among the founders of modern international law. These and many other honest men sincerely believed that the Indians had the capacity to live like civilized men, that colonization and Christianization could be totally peaceful, and that encomienda—the source of so much cruelty—should be abolished.

In 1512 the first laws trying to protect the Indians were promulgated; in 1518–1519 the first plans for nonviolent colonization were ready and in 1537–1550 they were introduced experimentally in Verapaz (a portion of present Guatemala). These plans and experiments eventually failed in the face of harsh colonial realities, but they did accomplish something positive: They convinced the Spanish kings of their moral obligation to do their best to build a colonial society in which Indians and immigrants could live together in peace and justice.

Meanwhile small groups of friars were sent to the New World to evangelize the Indians. Franciscans, Dominicans, and Augustinians went to New Spain (which got the cream of the crop) from 1523 on and to Peru after 1534. Their initial enthusiasm was as great as their ignorance of the Indian world. To the horror of modern archaeologists, they destroyed temples and idols by the hundreds in order to extirpate "false" religions, which they considered to be the work of Satan. They did their best to approach the Indians and convert them, but early failures and superficial successes soon proved the difficulty of their task. Because they had to learn native languages, they prepared the first Amerindian grammars and dictionaries. In order to indoctrinate the Indians, they tried to resettle them in missions, where the friars acted not only as missionaries but also as builders, community rulers, teachers of European agricultural and artisan techniques, and economic managers. They sincerely liked their simple, humble, obedient mission Indians and occasionally idealized them in a religious version of the *bon sauvage* glorified by the enlightened philosophers of eighteenth-century Europe. And they resented the presence of lay Spaniards, whose behavior contradicted their religious teachings. The most dedicated friars ended by embracing a providentialist interpretation of history: that the discovery and conquest had been a mere instrument of God to open the New World to its true destiny as a new Christendom consisting entirely of holy missionaries and angelic Indians. Thus their Christian universalism had nothing to do with European imperialism.

The utopian dreams of these idealists were never realized. The Crown was ready to finance and support evangelization, but only as a part of Iberianization. The early Franciscan plans for a native clergy, the college of Santiago Tlatelolco in Mexico, and other attempts to develop an Indian Christian elite in New Spain were abandoned. Moreover, when Fray Bernardino de Sahagún planned and directed (1540–1569) the compilation of linguistic, historical, and ethnological information about pre-Hispanic Mexico, his work was considered suspect and was sent to Spain for careful scrutiny. Missionary work was gradually confined to frontier regions, where the friars finally compromised with Hispanicization and allowed protective military garrisons and laymen near their settlements. The early missionaries, religious counterparts of the conquerors, belonged like them to the Middle Ages: Like spiritual conquerors, they went to the New World to build a terrestrial paradise and failed to fulfill their dream.

The network of frontier missions remained viable, however, and new religious orders arrived to reinforce it. The most important among them was the Society of Jesus. The Jesuits were the first such order to arrive in Brazil (1549), but they did not enter the Spanish colonies until 1568–1572. In 1607 they founded their missions in Paraguay; these came closest to the missionary ideal and epitomized the system's assets and shortcomings. Access to these missions was strictly limited to Indians and Jesuit missionaries and the missions constituted an idyllic, secluded world where the Indians lived in peace, obtained economic surpluses, manned their own military units for self-defense, and accepted the tutelage of the Jesuits. They thus became overprotected, perpetual minors who were unable to help themselves when the Jesuits were expelled from Spanish America in 1767.

THE ROYAL BUREAUCRACY

The Spanish colonial administration was from the beginning highly centralized at the top. The king was at its head, initially assisted by an agent in Seville. After 1503 a Board of Trade (*Casa de Contratación*) was in charge of navigation, trade inspection, and customs collection (in Portugal, a similar *Casa da India* or India House dealt with Asian trade only). In 1524 a colonial council (*Consejo de Indias*) was established in the Spanish court to assist the king, soon assuming full administrative, judicial, and fiscal duties, as well as the exercise of the *Patronato*. In contrast with this early centralization, the Portuguese king granted jurisdiction in colonial affairs to his existing political, economic, and ecclesiastic councils. The administration of the Asian colonies was not centralized until 1604; in 1643 it was expanded into an Overseas Council (*Conselho Ultramarino*), and finally took Brazil under its authority. These differences accounted for a more complex and better-organized public administration in rapidly developing Spanish America as opposed to a loose, less well-defined, and poorly controlled system in slowly developing Brazil. Nevertheless, both colonial administrations sprang from the same traditions and institutions; their differences were not in substance but in detail and sophistication.

Iberian colonial administration was performed by two hierarchies corresponding to the exercise of spiritual and political power. Ecclesiastic hierarchies took precedence over everyone but the Pope in matters of faith, doctrine, morals, and sacerdotal discipline; in other matters they were accountable to the king as patron of the Church. Political power, delegated by the king, was exercised by the metropolitan councils mentioned earlier, and by four different colonial bureaucracies. One, the government, was global in character and general in its duties; the other three were specialized and required professional training: the courts, the exchequer, and the army. The top political institutions in the Spanish colonies were the viceroyalties, one in Mexico from 1535 on, another in Lima after 1551; the viceroy was the personal representative of the king (and, as such, vice patron of the Church) and had the highest position in each colonial bureaucracy as governor of vast territories, honorary judge, paymaster general of the exchequer, and military commander. Such an accumulation of jobs was intended to enhance his prestige and authority, which was underlined by a military guard, a palatial residence, and a courtly life adequate to his rank. The highest administrator in Brazil at the time was a governor general in São Salvador de Bahia. From 1549 on he was the effective ruler of the captaincy of Bahia and military commander of Brazil.

Each Spanish viceroyalty included a number of governorships, each presided over by a governor as political ruler and provincial judge; if the governor had no legal training, justice was administered by his deputy professional judge. In the most important governorships the governor was also captain general, with full military powers. The governors were subordinate to their viceroy, but only nominally so if communications with Spain were easier or shorter than with the viceregal capital, as was the case with Venezuela and Río de la Plata (Buenos Aires). A total of thirty-four governorships existed in Spanish America, plus one in the Philippines. Their Portuguese equivalents were the captaincies, which remained as territorial divisions when the original proprietary captaincies had been reincorporated to the Crown. Each was ruled by a civilian governor.

Smaller territorial divisions in Spanish America were called corregimientos and ruled by *corregidores de españoles,* who had political and judicial authority within their provinces or districts. Rural districts with large Indian populations were under the rule of *corregidores de indios.*

The administration of justice at high levels was a very specialized task. Eleven *audiencias* were successively established in Spanish America and one in Manila as the highest courts of appeal in their respective districts. (The Brazilian counterpart in Bahia operated in 1609–1626 and was not reestablished until 1652.) Each *audiencia* consisted of several *oidores,* or senior Crown judges, plus a number of minor employees. Their verdicts were final in most cases but could sometimes be appealed to the *Consejo de Indias* as a supreme court. In Brazil, Crown judges of lower status also served as full-time specialized administrators of justice. At lower levels, down to the nonprofessional local justices of the peace, judicial power was exercised by the political rulers, as stated above.

The administration of the exchequer was also a separate, specialized operation. In Spanish America a number of regional offices were created, each with a minimum of three officers who were responsible for the accounting and custody of the treasury. The viceroy or governor acted as paymaster general. In Brazil the administration of the royal treasury was chaotic for a long time, except in the seaports where the customs collected most of the public revenue. In due course, however, a paymaster general and a board of revenue created a semblance of order.

The fourth specialized branch of the colonial administration was the military establishment. In Brazil the general governorship in Bahia was patterned after the Portuguese military governorship; the military commander of each captaincy reported to the governor general. In most of Spanish America, on the other hand, military organization was almost nonexistent. The viceroys' guards, few in number, were the only military units with high social prestige, good professional training, and true efficiency. A number of professional garrisons existed in key seaports, manning permanent fortifications to defend against outside attacks. On the frontiers scattered outposts with minimal garrisons were supplemented, when the occasion arose, by improvised private troops formed by local landlords and their employees. The landlords were sometimes granted honorary military rank, which boosted their social prestige and rewarded them for their free services. Governorships located at vital strategic points were given to professional soldiers, who acted as military governors (and therefore as commanders of all the garrisons within their districts) as well as civilian governors. Cuba and Chile were also administered in this way after 1573.

Although theoretically the four bureaucracies—government, justice, exchequer, and military—were independent from one another, we have seen how in practice many public jobs meant the exercise of power in two, three, or even all four of these administrations. This was one way of consolidating jobs and minimizing total salaries; contrary to general opinion, this meant a great deal of confidence in the loyalty and honesty of an appointee, qualities considered even more important than his professional qualifications. In the same spirit, employees in one bureaucracy were frequently given temporary or permanent tasks in another. An outstanding example is that of the *oidores*. Their job was strictly the administration of justice, but because of their training and competence they were usually the best advisers a viceroy had at hand. They were therefore given many commissions and temporary tasks in other branches of the administration. At times the dean of an *audiencia* acted as governor and captain general (as in Chile in 1567–1573); *oidores* were sometimes sent to the provinces on special missions; the *audiencia* and the viceroy met with growing frequency as a council of state or board of public finances.

The authority vested in the metropolitan councils was not at all easy to enforce. In an effort to get information—as much and as accurate as possible—about the colonies, any administrative officer was allowed and even encouraged to write directly to the Court; the same was true of colonial cities and individuals. Through the resulting maze of reports, complaints, denunciations, suggestions, and mere gossip, the *Consejo* tried to guess the situation overseas and to solve the problems that arose by means of another maze of orders and laws, often contradictory. Efforts were made to classify and codify these laws, but the results were deplorable in the case of Brazil (the Philippine Code of 1603) and late in the case of Spanish

America (the Colonial Code was not ready until 1680).
Besides, communications were slow; it might take one or
two years to solve a problem arising in the colonies if a
decision had to be made in Europe. Moreover, the natural
tendency of the European administrators to generalize
orders and standardize practices clashed with the growing
regional variety overseas and made a number of laws
inapplicable in certain places.

To reconcile the system's authority and centralized decision making with the flexibility and decentralization indispensable at provincial and local levels, two practical devices
were developed. One consisted in allowing just enough
initiative, corruption, and even anarchy in the colonies to
obtain a workable compromise between the law and its
application; this device was applied mainly in Brazil. The
second was the Spanish-American formula *obedezco, pero
no cumplo*, which made it possible for colonial officers to
suspend the enforcement of orders. By saying "I obey,"
the officer acknowledged that his superior, if well informed,
would never err; by saying "I do not execute," he assumed
the responsibility of postponing obedience until he could
inform his superior about all the circumstances and thereby
make possible a revised decision. In this way a certain balance between superior orders from Spain and local pressures in the colonies was maintained. The officer applied
the formula at his own risk because two elements of control were applied with relative success. One was a public
judicial review of the conduct of each royal officer at the
end of his term of office, which exposed illegal practices
and punished the guilty parties with fines, confiscations, or
imprisonment. The other was a secret inquiry carried out
by a judge, which in the event of serious denunciations
could be decreed at any time against one officer or a group
of them, in one locality or in a whole viceroyalty. More or
less parallel devices were applied in Brazil only sporadically
and with very limited success.

It is risky to summarize in general terms the operation
of the royal bureaucracies, but let us say that in Brazil it
was flexible, mostly inefficient, and considerably corrupt.

In Spanish America public administration was slow, cumbersome (there were frequent, serious conflicts between bureaucracies), subject to error, open to corruption, but remarkably efficient during the second half of the sixteenth century.

RELIGIOUS
INTEGRATION
The Church in Spanish America experienced deep changes during the late sixteenth century, reaching a turning point in the 1570s. The Council of Trent decided that no cleric might have jurisdiction over laymen or cure of souls unless he was subject to episcopal authority. This decree, accepted by the Crown in 1574, did much to change the colonial Church from a medieval, mainly missionary, pre-Tridentine church based on the regular clergy into a modern, post-Tridentine, centralized, autocratic Church under the authority of the bishops and based on a gradual dominance of the secular over the regular clergy. The friars—and their traditional, relatively democratic, exempt rule—were reduced to their frontier missions, convents, and parish work, now under the bishops' rule. Meanwhile the number of secular priests grew quickly, their organization improved, and a new spirit permeated the clergy: less fervor and more efficiency, less initiative and more controls, less attention to the frontiers and more to the growing cities. All this made the colonial Church less Indian, less colonial, and more Spanish than ever, and replaced the early colonial cleric—usually an apostolic friar—with the new parish priest, who was above all an organization man. In 1571 the Inquisition was installed in Spanish America (fortunately without jurisdiction over the Indians). Far less active than in Spain, the Holy Office eliminated some Jews and Protestants who made their way to the Indies but served primarily as a powerful instrument of discipline for the clergy, enhancing the authority of the bishops. After 1583 secular priests, if available, were preferred to friars as candidates for ecclesiastical benefices.

Meanwhile the Church had become rich. Since the early days it had received land and free Indian labor in generous amounts, plus subsidies from the State and the traditional total tax exemption. On top of that, innumerable private individuals not only paid their tithes but also offered spontaneous gifts in cash and real estate. They did so for two important reasons. First, a donation could be made on the conditon that the recipient community (convent, parish, or cathedral, for instance) grant the donor and his family certain honors (such as a burial place in a church or an inscription on the side of an altar) and intercessory prayers in specified quantities. In this way the social honor of giving to the Church was combined for these sincere believers with the assurance of enough prayers to get their souls and those of their loved ones out of Purgatory—a kind of "salvation insurance" deserving a substantial "premium" in cash or kind. Second, sins against the tricky Seventh Commandment could not be forgiven without restitution. A rich, old, repentant conqueror, for instance, could not locate all the Indians he had robbed, and even if he could he would dishonor himself by implicitly confessing to have been a robber; restitution made to the Church saved him this embarrassment and could be socially interpreted as generosity and piety. The same principles applied to everybody, from the unscrupulous merchant to the honest man who wanted to use his wealth as "manure to pile up in order to reach God from its top," as a medieval ascetic writer put it.

The cumulative wealth of the Church—and its active investment in land, real estate, mortgages, and loans—was legitimated on grounds of efficiency and charity (hospitals, orphanages, and schools operated by the Church needed money and property), the honor due to God (his temple is always modest for him, even if it is the biggest and richest building in town), and the need to add prestige to the Christian religion (the "ignorant" Indian would accept the new God as superior to his old ones if his temples were the most impressive). Realism (even a mystic soul needs food and shelter, the spiritual worker is entitled to his maintenance), expediency (money and organization are indispensable for apostolic work), and casuistry (to be poor in spirit is compatible with using things one does not own, but that one's Order does own) helped to accommodate the contradictions between the Church's wealth and the debilitated Christian tradition of disinterestedness and poverty.

A rich, socially prestigious, and politically influential Church attracted plenty of candidates to the ranks of the clergy. Although many followed genuine religious vocations, the clergy was also a promising career. Sons of the upper classes excluded by *mayorazgo* from family inheritances were nevertheless given an adequate education to be secular priests plus the right family connections to be promoted in due time to a rich urban parish, a living in a cathedral, or even a well-endowed bishopric (at the top of the ladder, the net income of the archbishop of Lima exceeded by far the salary plus perquisities of the viceroy). Naturally a priest's consecration and promotion depended largely on intellectual capacity, wisdom, and virtue, but education and recommendations evidently did the rest. For the offspring of the middle social groups, too, the clergy frequently offered the best possible future. And for the poor the lowest ranks of the clergy provided food, security, and the best vehicle for social mobility within the limits of social and racial barriers (which were broken in cases of extraordinary individual merits). Finally, a nunnery often served as a refuge for women.

The clergy offered many things to many people: peace, respectability, and time for the intellectually or artistically inclined to pursue their inclinations; action and opportunities for those with managerial talents; access to power for the power seekers; bread and respectability for the humble and hungry. All, of course, were supposed to pay a negative price in freedom and a positive one in obedience, discipline, work, and decorum. In this way the social environment gave the Church an unprecedented amount of capital and personnel, and a monolithic institutional solidity. Its monopoly of religion and its connection with the State through *Patronato* gave the Church considerable political power. Its authoritarian structure and stern discipline in matters of faith and obedience (under the Inquisition's vigilant eye) consolidated the clergy as a separate social sector and gave it a strong unity of purpose and action.

The Spanish-American Church consisted of five archbishoprics, thirty-one bishoprics (plus four in the Philippines), and one abbacy (in Jamaica, from 1515 to 1650), all established between 1511 and 1620. This structure was supplemented by the Provincials of the Orders, and had its strength in the network of cathedral chapters, convents, universities, colleges, hospitals, other charitable institutions, and parishes—down to the most remote missions and the poorest curates in Indian villages. Religious brotherhoods, lay associations, and family ties strongly linked the clergy with the rest of society.

The autocratic, paternalistic structure of the Church, its rigid orthodoxy, its emphasis on the "passive" Christian virtues (humility, patience, renunciation, obedience) over the "active" ones (love of freedom, hunger for justice, and the like) determined a kind of religiosity based on uncritical respect for authority, tradition, and routine. This big Church was not creative from a religious viewpoint (innovative thought was made dangerous by the Inquisition) but deeply conservative. The existing economic, social, and political situations were considered a "natural order of things" established or permitted by God, and any attempt to change or improve them beyond strict limits was arrogance and hence a capital sin. Poverty was regarded as an opportunity to exercise the virtues of patience on one side and charity on the other. And if justice could not be reached in this "Valley of Sorrow," it would be attained—perfect because administered by God himself—after death. Thus the hope of heaven made bearable any amount of suffering and lack of fulfillment.

The most desirable pattern of religious behavior was the one symbolized by John the Milkman in a later, but pertinent, story: Whenever he passed a church in the course of his work, he opened the door and said, looking at the main altar, "My Lord, here is John." John was the epitome of a humble religiosity, a blind, illiterate faith that was quoted as a perfect example of prayer and of feeling for the presence of God. No wonder the women, the least educated and most submissive, sentimental, and patient part of that society, were the deepest believers in and trustees of a social religiosity mainly expressed in ceremony, tradition, and custom, and almost never in creative thought or innovative behavior.

In Brazil the Church underwent a parallel, but far slower and more modest development. Until 1676 only one bishopric existed, established in 1551 with its see in Bahia. From 1591 on the Inquisition periodically sent commissioners to Brazil, but only a handful of suspects were shipped to Lisbon. Being relatively poor, the Church was not attractive as a career, and the comparatively small clergy was not powerful or influential (with the exception of a few Jesuits). The few, slowly expanding cities did not form an adequate framework for the concentration and growth of religious power. The Church was therefore less rigid and weaker, and this accounts for the survival of native, African, and non-Catholic European religious elements, as well as the later development of sects, superstitions, messianic movements, and highly syncretic religious practices.

POLITICAL INTEGRATION In a technical sense the Iberian territories in America were not colonies but part of the Castilian and Portuguese monarchies. Spanish America was formally incorporated to the Crown of Castile in 1519 by petition of the settlers, who did not want to take the risk of coming under foreign sovereignty (as could happen if the king, as personal lord of the Indies, decided to sell or transfer them to another monarch). Thus the colonies, as the kingdoms of the Indies, formed a number of political entities (New Spain, Peru, and so on), all constituting an integral and inalienable part of the Castilian Crown along with European kingdoms like León and Granada. It is true that the Indies never had a full political profile—for instance, the Cortes, or Parliament, never materialized despite some abortive attempts. But the same thing happened in the case of Granada, and even in Castile the Cortes gradually lost all importance during the sixteenth century as a result of the development of absolute rule. Castile grew, then, as a vast political entity comprising a number of kingdoms with one monarch and similar laws and institutions, though with a reasonable diversity of political status, custom, and usage at regional and local levels. Yet Castile itself was part of a broader political system that could be defined as a commonwealth or federation, supranational in character and heterogeneous in laws and traditions, having in common only its supreme ruler, the king. This federation gradually built up through interdynastic marriages and well-defined succession laws.

The federation was far from stable. In the days of Charles I (1517–1556), it was modeled on the medieval tradition of the Holy Roman Empire, duly enlarged and barely modernized; the whole was too large and diverse for efficient rule and was divided between the Spanish and Austrian branches of the Hapsburg Dynasty. Philip II (1556–1598) created with his inheritance a "Universal Monarchy," consisting of the Netherlands, the Crown of Aragón (with its kingdoms of Aragón proper, Sardinia, Sicily, and Naples), the Crown of Navarra, some minor territories, and the Crown of Castile. In 1580 the "Universal Monarchy" was rounded out by the succession of Philip II to the Crown of Portugal and its possessions in America, Asia, and Africa. To refer to this political entity as the Spanish Empire is a convenient but misleading simplification. Spain is an old Roman name for the Iberian Peninsula (*Hispania* in Latin, hence *España* and the term *españoles* or Spaniards for all Iberians, including the Portuguese until late in the seventeenth century), but as a national political entity Spain started to exist only in the eighteenth century.

For such a vast body the problems of rule and administration were immense. Each main political element had its own laws, borders, customs, and well-defined national interests; to harmonize them all to the interests of the ruling dynasty and its self-assumed international role required a difficult compromise between central authority and respect for national autonomy. Tensions and conflicts were frequent, even to the point of open nationalistic rebellions against the king. Two additional factors made the task even more difficult: First, Philip II established his court permanently in Castile and was deeply Castilianized; his rule was exercised by viceroys in the other kingdoms, and his political viewpoints moved progressively further from those of other sectors of his monarchy. Second, the arrogance typical of every large political system caused the Spanish empire to overextend itself and to decline under the burden of fantastic military expenses.

The system lasted for a while, largely thanks to the American silver production that made possible the deficit financing necessary to carry out Philip II's expensive ambitions. In 1565–1566, with the rebellion of the Netherlands, the "Universal Monarchy" encountered the danger of political disintegration. In the 1590s it started to crumble—deficit financing notwithstanding—under the burden of military expenses. In 1625, in an effort to increase resources and strengthen political control, plans were made to standardize and politically unify all of the kingdoms under Castilian law and administration—the one that gave the king the most authority. The result was the severe crisis of the 1640s, including broad nationalistic revolts that failed in the Crown of Aragón but succeeded in Portugal, which gained its independence. We will limit ourselves to the consequences in the New World.

As we have seen, a relatively efficient royal bureaucracy extended the authority of the king in the Spanish Indies during the second half of the sixteenth century. In the 1590s the bankrupt royal treasury, in a desperate move to obtain money, resorted to the device of rewarding with minor public jobs any qualified candidate willing to make a sizable cash donation to the king. During the seventeenth century this practice was expanded and transformed into an open sale of public offices. Limited at first to notary public and municipal jobs, the system gradually grew to include more important positions. These salable offices soon proliferated, and some were given in perpetuity in order to obtain more money; eventually they were awarded to the highest bidder and cynically negotiated without regard for the qualifications of the recipients. The system was rationalized as a kind of nonrefundable deposit made by the appointee as a guaranty of his performance, but there is no doubt about the corruption it engendered in public administration. The higher and more important jobs were never sold, of course, but continued to be conferred on the basis of personal honesty and qualifications.

The results of this system deserve to be summarized. It transformed the function of many public offices from a service into a naked business in which an initial cash investment was supposed to yield as high an economic benefit as possible; public administration thus became more than ever a source of exploitation. The remaining professional bureaucrats were demoralized by the sad fact that jobs that required a lifetime of work and dedication from them were given to anybody able to buy them, while inflation ate up an ever-increasing portion of their salaries. The ranks of the royal bureaucracy were greatly increased in order to satisfy the demands of job buyers and the king's need for cash, but this did not mean an increase in administrative effectiveness—the goal of many appointees was not to serve their country but to make money. Authority was weakened and flexibility increased to the point where it was possible to display open disregard for the law; the formula *obedezco, pero no cumplo* was interpreted in extreme cases as "I do want I want, paying lip service to the law."

Professional bureaucrats at top levels, surrounded by growing numbers of job-buyer subordinates, lost part of their effective power: They became less active as agents of the king and more as intermediaries between the well-entrenched vested interests and pressure groups in the colonies and the remote, less dedicated, and weaker kings in Madrid. The colonial economic and social elites were able to buy many offices and thereby acquired strong political leverage and even an ample degree of self-determination; they reached this goal gradually and peacefully, using money, while in other kingdoms open rebellion and bloody wars were necessary (and often failed) to preserve traditional decentralization and national identities. Because they were able to buy power, the rich criollos did not need to fight for it. They could even afford the luxury of remaining loyal to a distant and rather unobtrusive monarch, and to his political formula of "Universal Monarchy." Such loyalty had a price, paid in cash, subsidies, and taxes (very low compared to the tax burden of metropolitan Castile) but was well compensated by the international respectability enjoyed by the colonies as members of a European monarchy (even if it was already declining). The monarchy also offered a definite degree of military protection. This was not always very effective, but the colonies—economically dependent and militarily powerless—knew that without such protection they would have been up for grabs in the rapacious seventeenth-century Western world. The situation in Brazil did not differ much from that in Spanish America; the main distinction was that its cause was lack of development rather than the decadence of the royal bureaucracy.

# Chapter 5

# The Quest
# for
# Permanence

The Treaty of Tordesillas (1494) between Castile and Portugal was an early attempt to demarcate spheres of influence and to minimize conflicts. Castile agreed to respect Portuguese rights to the hemisphere east of a meridian located 370 leagues west of the Azores; Portugal acknowledged Castilian rights to the hemisphere west of this line. A possible source of disputes, mainly in Asia, could arise from the then-serious difficulty of determining longitude; this was settled in the Treaty of Zaragoza (1529).

THE IBERIAN MONOPOLY
The political union of Castile and Portugal (1580–1640) eliminated any further conflict during that period. English and French expeditions were organized after 1497 and 1524, respectively, to explore new sea routes between Europe and the Far East, but they failed in their attempts to find either a northwest or a northeast passage. This gave Portugal and Castile, at least for a certain time, a monopoly over their recently opened oceanic routes. But since these routes could not be kept secret forever, it was predictable that sooner or later the European expansion would become a source of international rivalries and conflicts.

The first to confront this problem from an academic viewpoint were a number of Castilian jurists, notably Francisco de Vitoria. In 1539 Vitoria formulated a universal law of nations, the initial step in the development of modern international law. He rejected the idea that either the Pope or the emperor was entitled to exercise temporal jurisdiction over alien princes or peoples, be they Christian, heathen, or infidel, and proclaimed the right of each nation to freedom and to peaceful trade and intercourse with every other nation. Fernando Vázquez de Menchaca, another Castilian jurist, elaborated on the principle of freedom of the seas, rejecting the idea that any nation was entitled to the monopoly over navigation in any ocean or part of it. These ideas were not welcome to the king (who maintained a monopolistic policy), and they began to fade away in 1568, when academic freedom and intellectual cosmopolitanism came to an end in Castile.

In 1608 a Dutch jurist, Hugo de Groot (better known by his Latinized name, Grotius), developed and popularized these ideas in his dissertation *Mare Liberum*, with the specific purpose of justifying the presence in the Far East of Dutch merchants competing with the Portuguese. In this way ideas on peaceful international coexistence were put to good use to rationalize conflicts but not to solve them. As usual, international relations developed on grounds of power and violence, not justice and peace. In consequence, the Iberians did their best to consolidate their initial colonies, and the latecomers did as much as they could to break the early Iberian monopoly of colonization and intercontinental trade. The subsequent conflicts were purely economic ones, though they were soon dignified with a veneer of legality, patriotism, and even religion. In turn, these factors tended to deepen economic antagonisms, making them more violent and bloody: To ruin or kill a "papist" had a touch of righteousness and glory for a Protestant, and the same went for a Catholic with respect to a "heretic."

Let us summarize how the Iberian monopoly quietly collapsed from within. We mentioned earlier that transatlantic trade grew moderately during the first half of the sixteenth century. This was to the benefit of Seville, the port singled out for traffic with the colonies. In 1543 the big merchants of Seville obtained the privilege of being legally incorporated into a merchant guild, which from then on exercised a monopoly over colonial trade. The large profits of these merchants and their city soon spread to most of Castile, strongly stimulating agricultural and industrial production. Andalusian wines and olive oil were sent to the colonies in large amounts; ships were built in Seville, but mainly in the shipyards of Bilbao and other seaports of northern Castile; textiles, weapons, and manufactures of many other kinds went from prosperous Castilian cities to the colonies via Seville.

This sudden prosperity created a number of problems. The unavoidable inflation produced by strong demand developed very soon. In 1556 high prices were related for the first time to the abundance of bullion brought from America, and from then on a handful of Castilian economists continued to write sensibly about economic problems and solutions. Unfortunately for their country, they were not then the political oracles that economists would become much later. Economic policy was based on two principles only: fiscal profit, or trying to maximize tax receipts for the royal treasury without killing the goose that laid the golden eggs, and expediency, or giving a sympathetic ear to complaints by merchants and consumers and providing the empirical solutions they desired.

In the early 1560s the booming production of the silver mines increased demand in the colonial markets to such an extent that it exceeded the immediate possibilities of Castilian production. Consumers in Europe complained about prices and even shortages of several products; consumers in the colonies, facing the same problems, resorted to contraband with foreign smugglers. The short-term solutions adopted then were based on expediency. The colonies were permitted and even encouraged to develop their own vineyards and olive groves. This they did, with prompt relief for wine and oil prices in Castile and long-term losses of colonial markets for Castilian wine and olive growers. To stabilize industrial prices, large imports of European manufactures were allowed in Castile (without protective tariffs to help infant Castilian industries), and bullion export licenses were granted to Castilian merchants to compensate for a quickly deteriorating balance of payments. The Netherlands, France, Northern Italy, and to a greater or lesser extent the rest of Western Europe benefited most from this economic policy. In a vain effort to preserve the colonial monopoly of Castile, foreign merchants were not allowed to trade with Spanish America.

But by then only a shadow of the monopoly remained. The nature of trade had altered because the colonies could use growing amounts of silver to pay for more diversified, sophisticated, and costly European manufactures. The latter came to Seville and Cádiz (the most important of the Sevillian outports), and exports to the colonies skyrocketed. The merchants of Seville developed a big agency and commission business, sending goods to Spanish America on behalf of merchant houses all over Europe. A few decades sufficed, however, for the ruin of Castilian industries, which had been prosperous until the 1550s. Merchants and manufacturers from the most economically developed regions of Europe, with enough capital resources to practice systematic "dumping," were able to avoid lowering home prices while at the same time capturing the Castilian market. Thus Spanish America made possible the sustained economic boom of the richest and most industrialized regions of Europe, whereas Castile, for lack of a sound economic policy at a critical point in its economic development, lost its best opportunity for industrialization.

Portugal's economic monopoly over Brazil was even more superficial than that of Castile over Spanish America. As we have seen, Dutch capital, marketing, and even ships were essential in the development of sugar production. A comparatively liberal system of transport and commerce thus limited the role of Portugal to that of administrator of the colony and middleman between Brazil and the richest regions of Western Europe.

The first Spanish-American colonies remained undisturbed for a while, their insignificance and remoteness protecting them from the cupidity of other Europeans. As soon as they started to feed a regular, rich trade route, however, they attracted the interest of European seamen. As early as 1507, two caravels were sent by the king to escort Spanish ships for the last leg of their homeward voyage. In 1521, with the outbreak of war with France, the merchants of Seville felt apprehensive enough to volunteer the financing of a naval squadron with the same purpose. In 1523, part of the booty of the conquest sent from New Spain was captured near the Azores by a French privateer. From then on the interest of many people in Western Europe was focused on the maritime lifeline of the Spanish Empire, endangering the Castilian monopoly almost from its beginning.

The dangers were of several kinds. The natural desire of foreign merchants and sailors to participate peacefully in the benefits of a new trade route, declared illegal by the Crown, gave rise to contraband. Piracy, too, was a fact of contemporary life: A ship had to be ready to fight or flee at any time. Piracy was a business for poor sailors who attacked vessels and whales for the same purpose—to make a living. Equivalent to banditry on land, piracy had a certain economic function; that is, it gave people from poor areas a way to participate in the wealth of the rich ones. Another danger lay in the fact that international wars in Europe were bound sooner or later to affect American waters and coasts. All the important naval battles were fought on European seas, of course, and until 1596 none took place between regular royal fleets in the New World; nevertheless, from the 1530s on war meant the presence in colonial seas of privateers eager to serve their king and themselves by attacking Spanish ships or coastal settlements. In many cases privateers and pirates were identical, royal letters of marque making the only difference.

Peaceful contraband consisted mainly of African slaves. From 1532 to 1580 the legal slave trade in the Caribbean was carried on by dealers who obtained royal licenses to import a specific number of slaves. Smuggling took several forms: forgery of licenses, import of more slaves than the permit allowed (if local officers could be bribed), and unlicensed trade. The dealers depended on Portuguese middlemen, who obtained most of the slaves on the coasts of Guinea and Angola. The Portuguese soon started their own trade from there to small, discrete harbors on the Spanish Main; with no tax or license to pay, they sold more cheaply than regular dealers and obtained from their Spanish customers hides, sugar, and later tobacco and silver. In 1595 the slave trade was legally established in Buenos Aires, which was allowed general trade with Brazil in 1602; this generated a contraband that grew during the seventeenth century and was able to divert substantial but unknown amounts of silver from Potosí. The Portuguese were forbidden by treaty to trade in Spanish America; hence, in an effort to escape notice, they were as quiet and cooperative as possible. Their Spanish customers welcomed them with delight, along with Flemish interlopers (subjects of the same king but foreigners on Castilian territory) and early French and English smugglers.

Through these channels Spanish America gradually developed its own commercial ties with Africa and Europe, getting slaves from the former, and manufactures from the latter. Because of the illegal and secretive nature of this business, its extent can only be guessed at. In 1567 navigation began between Mexico and the Philippines; its amount was modest at first, but no limitations were imposed upon it. Although navigation between Peru and Asia was forbidden and after 1571 only one galleon per year was authorized from Acapulco to Manila, in 1597 the amount of bullion illegally sent to the Philippines exceeded the total value of legal transatlantic trade in the same year. Thus Spanish America developed its own commerce with

Asia, bringing back, via Manila and Acapulco, large amounts of luxury manufactures, mainly silk. Part of the Asian silk was reexported from Acapulco to Peru and part to Spain until the 1640s.

It is clear, then, that Spanish America was bound to spontaneously develop a commercial system of its own, world-wide in scope and internally strengthened by growing intercolonial trade between Spanish-American regions with different and complementary production. The flow of official trade to Seville suffered in consequence. It was easy for the Sevillian merchants (among the most rapacious and short-sighted commercial oligarchies in history) to convince the king that they were all in the same boat: If the established colonial monopoly grew, Seville would get more benefits and the king more tax revenue; with contraband increasing in the colonies and trade with Asia developing, Seville would channel less bullion and the king would collect less in taxes.

The Crown was thereby persuaded to enforce the official monopoly more strongly. Trade between Buenos Aires and Brazil was forbidden in 1618. After 1597, traffic between Acapulco and Manila was drastically limited. Navigation between Mexico and Peru was reduced after 1604 and forbidden in 1631. Briefly, intercolonial trade was either suppressed or reduced to a minimum. The same went for navigation between Spanish America and the rest of the world, except Seville and its outports. Thus an all-out effort was made to preserve the vested monopolistic interests of merchants and monarch. Confiscations and big fines were decreed against Spanish smugglers and their customers in Spanish America, and foreign smugglers were treated as privateers or pirates.

As a result of this harsh policy, a number of foreign smugglers became pirates (both jobs had been made equally dangerous, and the latter was more profitable). The Spanish Americans developed a growing disregard for the king's arbitrary rules, successfully circumvented them, and turned the purchase of smuggled goods—initially an economic convenience—into a game with some of the danger, excitement, and virtuosity of a bullfight. Thus they invented a Hispanic way of life in which the unreasonable strictness and weight of law and authority were made bearable by its lack of enforcement and a peculiar kind of defensive, anarchic unruliness that has often been inaccurately called "Spanish individualism." In political as well as economic and administrative aspects, there was evidence of an incipient opposition between society and state, a divergence of interests between the nations and peoples of the "Universal Monarchy" on one side and the king, his dynastic policies, and the privileged ruling elites on the other. The independence of Holland, Portugal, and Spanish America were some of the many political crises of the Spanish monarchy that stemmed from this root.

While Spanish America welcomed peaceful smugglers and benefited from their trade, it always hated and feared pirates and privateers. Piracy of the transatlantic trade started in the eastern Atlantic between the Azores and the Iberian Peninsula, where ships coming back from America or Asia were awaited and pounced on, forming a number of good catches. During the reign of Charles I (1517–1556), wars between Spain and France were frequent; hence most of the pirates were French privateers. In the 1530s, when Castilian fleets made the eastern Atlantic too risky for them, they started operations in the remote Caribbean, dividing their efforts between surprise attacks on Spanish ships in the Straits of Florida and plundering expeditions against defenseless coastal settlements. During the 1560s English sailors also entered the American scene, giving up their initial business of peaceful smuggling for the more rewarding ones of privateering during the years of Anglo-Spanish war and piracy in peacetime, the distinction being purely judicial and scarcely relevant.

It is time now to evaluate the results of the contest and the achievements (as of 1610) of each party involved: the king, Castile, the Spanish colonies, and the foreign plunderers who, irrespective of national origin, had the same goals and strategy. In general terms the Hapsburg king was the winner. He was vitally interested in the punctual arrival at Seville of American bullion in the largest possible amounts in order to finance his expensive dynastic policy of hegemony in Europe. He regarded America and the Atlantic as the backyard of his monarchy, where worries and expenses should be minimal. He therefore channeled the lion's share of the American bullion through Seville, organized heavily protected convoy navigation (using galleons—large, specialized fighting ships with heavy broadside armament fully developed in the 1550s), and fortified the main ports of call of the silver fleets (Havana, Veracruz, Cartagena, and to a lesser extent Portobello and Panama on the Isthmus). As a result the fleets sailed without meaningful losses and with remarkable regularity, enabling the king to finance the best army in the contemporary world, the endeavor of Counter Reformation, and the many other glories of the Spanish Hapsburgs.

The Spanish nations, mainly Castile, were the big losers, with only the temporary exception of the merchant clique of Seville and its foreign associates. Castilian national interest was in the Atlantic and overseas, not in continental Europe, and it could have been defended from the bastion of the Pyrenees as effectively as England later defended the English Channel. The vital tools for lasting supremacy on the Atlantic and the eastern Pacific were available, and the appropriate strategy was planned at the right time. This consisted of a large, permanent Atlantic fleet (1524), strong naval squadrons based in Seville and Santo Domingo (1552), a big naval base in the Scilly Islands (1573), a Peruvian-based fleet in the Pacific, and the like. But all of these elements either remained in the planning stage or were underdeveloped or soon discontinued for lack of money (the money was available too but was spent for dynastic, not national, purposes). In the late sixteenth century, as we have seen, Castilian industries were either dying or dead. Among them was shipbuilding, declining for lack of the subsidies and protection it had received in former and happier times. Daring Castilian teenagers dreamed no longer of becoming pilots at sea, but captains

in the infantry. With the untimely death of Pedro Menéndez de Avilés (1574), the tradition of great admirals—
confined for decades to defensive, not aggressive, tasks—
died too. The concentration of colonial trade in Seville,
initially a sound policy, was senselessly prolonged when
bigger ships made the port obsolete. Thus the vested interests of a local coterie succeeded in suppressing competition
among Spanish ports for colonial trade and minimizing
contacts between Spaniards on both sides of the Atlantic.
The old and new territories of Castile drifted apart and
lost their early feeling of belonging to a single kingdom
and national community.

As a consequence of royal policy, Spanish America lost
out too. Efficient protection of the fleets and their ports
in the Caribbean was good for American silver when it
was already in European hands, but this left most of the
coastal cities at the mercy of aggressors. Minimizing or
suppressing by law local, intercolonial, and transoceanic
trade was good for the monopoly but went against the
interest of Spanish America in wider contact and intercourse with the rest of the world, which would have been
profitable in economic terms and creative from a cultural
viewpoint. Colonial Buenos Aires would have died of economic suffocation if isolationist traffic restrictions had
been strictly obeyed. Most of the Caribbean islands and
coasts were not extensively settled or developed, mainly
for climatic reasons, but restrictive laws on trade and
navigation helped minimize Spanish settlement, depopu-
late some settled areas, and make the Caribbean a dangerous door to the Spanish-American world—which
consequently tended to grow self-contained and relatively
isolated. Traffic regulations thus transformed the eastern
Pacific from a springboard into a barrier, from a Spanish
preserve until 1580 into a field for foreign predators
thereafter.

What the colonies needed and asked for was permanent
protection of the seas and help and encouragement in
developing a shipbuilding industry. Of both they received
too little, too late. Havana, Guayaquil, and other shipyards

built enough ships and repair facilities for the fleets, but they were not encouraged to do much more. The cheapest and most effective defense against foreign raiders would have been to respond in kind, granting all willing Spanish seamen letters of reprisal and full rights to any booty they obtained as privateers; this was not done until 1674, when Spanish navigation outside the fleets was already reduced to almost nothing. The very powerful reason for this laxness was that allowing plenty of ships in the colonies with freedom of movement would have increased contraband, to the detriment of the interests of the king and the merchants who benefited from the official monopoly. It is true that the king provided some relief in the form of minor coastal fortifications and garrisons (enough to discourage isolated pirates but not full-fledged attacks by squadrons of privateers), coast guard patrols (such as the galleys of Cartagena), and even true fleets with permanent defensive tasks (like the fleet established in 1582 to protect the eastern Caribbean). However, these fleets, active and very successful when the situation was critical, were reduced in size, left to rot for lack of crews, or simply disbanded as soon as the aggressors had been forced to flee; this lack of continuity, due to lack of money (generously invested in infantry for the battlefields of Europe) provided a temporary respite but not an effective and permanent solution.

Pirates not backed by European nations were simply a nuisance. Their historical importance consists in proving the lack of defenses of the Spanish colonies, thus encouraging non-Iberian attacks and later colonizations in the Caribbean, in which they served as forerunners, cannon fodder, and early settlers. During the seventeenth century they grew in number and notoriety and were known locally as buccaneers, freebooters, or filibusters. Although they were later idealized as romantic anarchists, they excelled mainly in robbing and killing with fanatic anti-Spanish fervor. More important were the privateers backed by European powers. They totally failed in their ambitious goal of attacking and establishing permanent military garrisons in a few key Spanish Caribbean ports and on the Isthmus of Panama. If successful, this plan would have broken the Spanish communication and supply system, depriving Spain of the means to make war in Europe and opening Spanish America to French or English exploitation. (The plan was conceived by the French in 1555, and Francis Drake tried to carry it out in 1585.) The episodic success of the privateers consisted in plundering expeditions that yielded positive results in booty and prestige but no permanent territorial or strategic advantages before the 1630s. On the negative side, their brutal aggressiveness soon gave rise in Latin America to a lasting xenophobia that was one of the most important factors in the preservation of Latin American cultural and historical identity.

THE DUTCH CHALLENGE
Before the 1610s the concerted efforts of France, England, and the buccaneers failed to make territorial gains of any consequence in the New World. The French, after an unsuccessful attempt in 1534–1536, founded (1603) a remote and insignificant settlement in *Nouvelle France*, or French Canada. A venture in Brazil—a modest foothold in Río de Janeiro (1555), the wishful beginning of a *France Antarctique*—was a disaster, and the Huguenot colony of *Caroline* (1564) in northern Florida, a potential danger to Spanish navigation in the Straits of Florida, was ruthlessly destroyed by Menéndez de Avilés. The English, who failed in a badly chosen settlement on Guiana (1604) and started a marginal colony in Virginia (1607), spent their resources on plundering expeditions rather than colonization. The end of the Iberian monopoly over settlement in the New World was a result not of external pressures but of conflict within the Spanish Empire.

The already-mentioned tensions between the "dynasticism" of the king and the incipient modern nationalism of his kingdoms were frequently manifested in discontent and open rebellion from the very beginning of the Hapsburg rule. It all started in Spain with the civil wars of 1519–1523 in Castile and Aragón. The king, with the assistance of the nobility, crushed both rebellions and carried out a merciless repression that put all the power in the hands of king and nobles for a very long time. The repercussions of these conflicts in the New World have not been systematically explored, but the existing data suggest that emigrants fleeing the repression—true political exiles coming from the urban middle groups—were responsible for the best and most constructive accomplishments of the "world of the conquerors" described in chapter 1.

The second and crucial episode of rebellion took place in the Burgundian-Hapsburg kingdom of the Netherlands, a far more sensitive and dangerous location than Castile or Aragón for many reasons. First, it was the richest, most densely populated, and most economically developed region of the monarchy. Second, it was the domain most loosely attached to it; the king, though respected, had not yet won the people's blind devotion as a sacred symbol, something he already enjoyed in Castile. Third, militant Calvinism had made deep inroads, adding the potential of a religious dimension to any serious political or economic conflict. Fourth, the nobility was in general more inclined to side with the rebels than with the king. Fifth and most important, hostile neighboring powers like France and England were close enough to offer the Flemish rebels sanctuary, economic aid, and military assistance—which they did, thereby transforming a domestic conflict into an international one.

Philip II knew all this, and in 1567 sent the third Duke of Alba with a corps of elite troops so efficient and well-organized as an army of occupation that it left Italy with some two thousand prostitutes organized in battalions and companies. From then until the Twelve Years' Truce—reached in 1609, when both sides in the conflict were exhausted—forty-two years of cruel, bloody war provided plenty of opportunities for the king's troops to prove not only their competence and heroism but also the political sterility of military rule and the oft-forgotten lesson about the incongruity of trying to reach political goals with military means. The fighting did not end in 1609, however, and Dutch independence was not formally acknowledged until the Treaty of Münster (1648). But for all practical purposes Dutch nationalism was already victorious in the northern part of the Netherlands in 1609.

From our viewpoint the crucial event in that protracted conflict was the closing of Iberian ports to rebel trade and ships in 1594. This decision, intended as an economic reprisal, badly backfired because it broke the symbiotic economic relationship between the Netherlands and Portugal, to the detriment of the latter as the weaker element in the system, and impelled the Dutch to go directly to the sources of their trade with the Portuguese.

In 1595 the Dutch made their first voyage to the Far East in search of spices that could no longer be brought from Lisbon. The Dutch East India Company, a big, modern, chartered corporation, was organized in 1602 for the spice trade. In 1600 salt for fish preservation and other industrial uses—no longer coming from southern Portugal —was being harvested in Araya, a desolate bay on the coast of Venezuela, where an enclosed lagoon and a torrid climate produced big deposits of salt. Since the commercial Dutch mind would have considered it nonsensical to dispatch ships to Araya in ballast, they carried European manufactures to be sold on the Spanish Main, rounding out with tobacco and hides their cargoes of salt for the voyage home. Shortly after they were expelled from Araya by the Spaniards, they founded the settlement of Surinam, or Dutch Guiana (1602–1603). Then, as soon as the truce with the king of Spain was over, they organized the Dutch West India Company (1621). This was a rather unstable combination of business and religion—crusading Calvinists were influential in the corporation's management—so the final results were more spectacular than profitable.

In 1628 an admiral of the Dutch West India Company, the very able Pieter Heyn, accomplished the unprecedented feat of capturing a Mexican silver fleet at the harbor of Matanzas, Cuba. Although this was an isolated success at sea against the Spaniards, the amount of the booty permitted further endeavors and made sensational news. The commander of the captured fleet was punished as a scapegoat by the Hapsburg king, though his policies had neglected and undermined the old naval supremacy of Castile.

After an initial blunder came the conquest of the sugar business: In 1630 the building of New Holland started with the attack on Pernambuco and the subsequent conquest of northeastern Brazil, where the Dutch regime lasted until 1654. To consolidate their sugar empire, the Dutch took Elmina in 1638 and Luanda, Angola, in 1641, thus providing their recently acquired sugar plantations with African slaves in an economical way. After 1634, with the occupation of Curaçao, they established the first permanent entrepôt for large-scale foreign contraband in the Spanish Caribbean.

In the 1620s the Dutch opened a new era in the colonization of the New World by introducing their astute, modern form of commercialism, which made the commercial capitalism of the Iberians look old-fashioned and inefficient. Conquests and battles notwithstanding, the real heroes of those years were boats and crews, banks and merchants. The flyboat, a great innovation in naval technology, was invented in Dutch shipyards during the 1590s. Cleverly and cheaply built, this efficient freighter gave Holland mastery over the bulk-cargo trade as well as a profitable item for export to other countries. The flyboat was essential in the Caribbean because it provided interlopers and buccaneers with an instrument of contact with Europe. This gave the buccaneers for the first time, at reasonable cost and in adequate amounts, men, supplies, and good markets for their produce. The earliest French and English settlements in the Caribbean (St. Christopher in 1622, Guadeloupe and Martinique in 1635, and others) depended for a time on Dutch shipping. Without it they might not have survived during the first critical decades. Finally, the Amsterdam Exchange Bank and the Loan

Bank, founded in 1609 and 1614, respectively, were essential for the speedy settlement of debts among merchants and for money loans.

The Dutch accomplishment had its limits; its apogee was short-lived. The Treaty of The Hague (1596), mustering enough power to destroy the Spanish monarchy in a time of diplomatic isolation for Philip II, was dismantled by France and England when they abandoned Holland and signed separate peace treaties with Spain in 1598 and 1604, respectively. The English Navigation Acts of 1651 revealed an anti-Dutch attitude that led to the Anglo-Dutch wars of 1652–1654 and 1665–1667. The buildup of English naval power was fatal for Holland, which depended on the English Channel as a narrow doorway to its world-wide sea trade; the Dutch also used English waters for fishing. In 1655, when England was able to occupy Jamaica and for the first time successfully blockade the southern coast of Spain, it became clear that Holland had lost momentum and England could emerge as the great naval and colonial power of the years to come.

AMERICA AND THE WORLD UNTIL 1650
Until 1650 European expansion in Africa and Asia was limited to the seas, coastal enclaves, and islands. All of the settlements in these areas played a marginal role in terms of cultural intercourse though their economic activities were important. Relations between America on one side and Asia and Africa on the other were also limited. One ship per year formed a tiny bridge between Mexico and the Philippines, the latter consisting of a handful of Spanish settlements surrounded by an Oriental world almost impenetrable but for economic contacts. Spanish America received slightly more immigrants from Africa than from Spain, while African immigration to Brazil was large in absolute numbers and even greater as a percentage of the total population. Nevertheless, the African cultural impact was small until 1650: In urban areas, the assimilation of uprooted and scattered African slaves was only a matter of time (a very short period when the slaves came from Europe and were already more or less Europeanized); in

rural areas, the concentration of blacks, mainly on sugar plantations, had a certain cultural impact in colonial societies. This was probably limited to folkloric and minor structural aspects until the massive development of the slave trade in the eighteenth century.

In contrast with these small cultural contacts among continents and civilizations, Europe and America developed a steady intercourse that made their destinies appear inseparable. This development is expressed today in the nebulous concepts of "Western World" (which tends to overlook Latin America, often thrown into the odds-and-ends basket labeled "Third World") and "Atlantic Civilization." The latter is a more comprehensive term but nevertheless minimizes, even ignores, many regional differences; moreover, it refers to a historical reality that reached its peak between 1870 and 1960, and has been declining slowly but steadily since then. In fact, the cosmopolitanism resulting from easy world-wide communications and the diffusion of the same material culture (now European only in historical origin) is being more than compensated by the differentiating and divisive role of a generalized nationalism that is deepening and growing along multiplied international borders and even inside them.

It is not easy to assess the unique relationship between Europe and America. According to the traditional Eurocentric interpretation, the latter is historically a mere creation or extension of the former. Recent reassessments inspired by enthusiastic archaeologists and anthropologists tend, on the other hand, to take a favorable view of pre-colonial American civilizations and often a very harsh one of the European colonial legacy. Both are, of course, one-sided interpretations; the most unbalanced, however, is the romantic view that has developed mainly in Mexico and tries to directly link the pre-Hispanic past with the present national culture, treating the colonial period as an oppressive transitional period. The truth is that the aboriginal civilizations did not survive the colonial era at all: Their political structures disappeared with the conquest, their social and economic profiles were deeply altered by the decline of the Indian populations and the expansion of a capitalistic economy, and their nonmaterial culture was decisively changed by Christianization and colonial administration. Some Indian groups became extinct, while others remained isolated in marginal areas; the last of these are now either extinct or approaching total extinction or assimilation. What now survives of the Indian world may be found in a number of mestizo Spanish-Indian cultures, which emerged during the colonial period and are now disintegrating under the pressure of modern, industrial, urban civilization.

In a broad and very suggestive way, the New World has been regarded by a Texan and historian, W. P. Webb, as the "great frontier" of Europe. In his view the discovery and occupation of America suddenly altered the European ratio among three factors: population, available land, and capital. This provided Europe with a sudden economic surplus that made possible four centuries of boom. By about 1900 the frontier lands were already populated and the ratio between population and land in the Western World was stabilizing and would soon decline. Thus between 1500 and 1900 the great American frontier transformed and enhanced a Western civilization that until then had remained relatively static in Europe and was considerably provincial in extent and outlook.

Webb's interpretation has the merit of emphasizing the interaction between Europe and America, and providing a comprehensive frame of reference for four centuries of Western history. However, it gives the New World a central, decisive role that it did not actually have. The rapid, world-wide economic consequences of the early colonization have been summarized, and so has its demographic impact. A list of American goods formerly unknown in the Old World, from tobacco to potatoes and quinine, would include hundreds of items. But all of these contributions did not change the economic evolution of Europe, though they certainly acted as stimulants. From a political standpoint, we have seen how in the 1620s America was already integrated into the European political and diplomatic system and how power struggles in Europe acquired a genuine transatlantic extension, but the center of power and decision making remained in Europe. And from a social perspective, we have described the transplantation of European patterns and systems to America, where they were adapted and modified but never drastically changed.

To explain in a few words the historical intercourse between Europe and America, and to assess the role of each, let us say that colonial America had a submissive, subordinate role while Europe had an active, dominant role. America was a challenge and a trophy. Europe went overseas to face the former and to take the latter, to "unite the world and give to those strange lands the form of our own."(According to a Castilian humanist writing in 1528, this was the purpose of the Spaniards, beginning in 1493 with the second voyage of Columbus.) In economic and political terms the American challenge was immediately accepted and the trophy quickly won. As an intellectual challenge, however, America was a more difficult prize. Europeans knew something about Africa and Asia, but America was outside the range of their past experience and normal expectations for the future. This is why the European effort to understand the New World and to integrate it into the mental framework of a classical-Judeo-Christian tradition was slow, though remarkably and surprisingly effective. It started in the days of Columbus with the attentive observation of explorers and the curiosity of immigrants and with the careful descriptions given by the early Spanish chroniclers like Gonzalo Fernández de Oviedo, the naturalist and physician Francisco Hernández, and many others; it developed in spite of the slowness with which the wealth of early observations and descriptions was disseminated throughout Europe. (In those days of slow communications and limited use of printing, most of the studies and treatises written were unknown by the masses and not published until recent times.)

By the end of the sixteenth century, a clear comprehension of the New World had finally emerged in the writings of José de Acosta, Diego Durán, Juan de Tovar, and others. It is of secondary importance whether they had the right or wrong idea of America. The essential thing is that, pursuing it, they relied less and less on tradition and authority, more and more on free scientific inquiry. Thus they paved the way for an intellectual revolution in Europe and reinforced a linear, progressive interpretation of history as opposed to the cyclical one stressing the rise and fall of civilizations. All this gave Europe the self-confidence, optimism, and arrogance that later crystallized in the accomplishments and philosophy of full-fledged European imperialism.

Sixteenth-century Europeans were also the first to see and criticize the negative aspects of that imperialism, even at its incipient stage (as Bartolomé de Las Casas and others did so bravely), as well as to propose new legal and ethical principles of freedom and mutual respect in human relations at both the personal and collective levels (as Francisco de Vitoria and others did so intelligently and compassionately).

Finally, America was the place where Europeans who cared for high adventure and feared nothing projected their impossible dreams and toiled to reach their unreachable utopias: conquerors who tried to rebuild a feudal society already dead in Europe; missionaries who wished to create a perfect Christendom; those among the colonial bureaucrats who sincerely believed in and honestly labored for the rule of just law; emigrants who went overseas looking for bread, peace, and opportunity in exchange for hard work, or for justice, self-esteem, and freedom as political or spiritual exiles. Whether or not they succeeded or failed in their quest, it matters even more in historical terms that they tried so hard. In J. H. Elliott's subtle and beautiful words, "if America nurtured Europe's ambitions, it also kept its dreams alive. And perhaps dreams were always more important than realities in the relationship of the Old World and the New."*

---

* J. H. Elliott. *The Old World and the New, 1492–1650.* Cambridge: Cambridge University Press, 1970. P. 104.

# Bibliography

GENERAL

Boxer, Charles R. *The Portuguese Seaborne Empire: 1415–1825.*
New York: Alfred A. Knopf, Inc., 1969.

Diffie, Bailey W. *Latin American Civilization: Colonial Period.*
New York: Octagon Books, 1967 (reprint).

*Gibson, Charles. *Spain in America.* Harper Torchbooks. New
York: Harper & Row, Inc., 1967.

Griffin, Charles C. (ed.). *Latin America: A Guide to the Historical Literature.* Austin: University of Texas Press, 1971.

Humphreys, R. A. *Latin American History: A Guide to the
Literature in English,* 2d ed. New York: Oxford University
Press, 1960.

*Parry, J. H. *The Age of Reconnaissance.* Mentor Books. New
York: The New American Library, Inc., 1964.

———. *The Spanish Seaborne Empire.* New York: Alfred A.
Knopf, Inc., 1966.

Payne, Stanley G. *A History of Spain and Portugal.* 2 vols. Madison: University of Wisconsin Press, 1973.

CHAPTER 1

*Kirkpatrick, F. A. *The Spanish Conquistadores.* Meridian Books.
New York: World Publishing Co., 1962 (reprint).

Lockhart, James. *Spanish Peru, 1532–1560: A Colonial Society.*
Madison: University of Wisconsin Press, 1968.

*Morison, Samuel Eliot. *Christopher Columbus, Mariner.* New
York: The New American Library, Inc., 1956.

*Nowell, Charles E. *The Great Discoveries and the First Co-
lonial Empires,* rev. ed. Ithaca: Cornell University Press, 1965.

*Padden, R. C. *The Hummingbird and the Hawk: Conquest and
Sovereignty in the Valley of Mexico, 1503–1541.* Harper Colo-
phon Books. New York: Harper & Row, Inc., 1970.

Verlinden, Charles. *The Beginnings of Modern Colonization.*
Ithaca: Cornell University Press, 1970.

Zavala, Silvio. *New Viewpoints on the Spanish Colonization of*

*Available in paperback.

**CHAPTER 2**

*America.* Philadelphia: University of Pennsylvania Press, 1943.

Bakewell, P. J. *Silver Mining and Society in Colonial Mexico: Zacatecas, 1546–1700.* Cambridge Latin America Studies. New York: Cambridge University Press, 1971.

Borah, Woodrow. *New Spain's Century of Depression.* Ibero-Americana, vol. 35. Berkeley: University of California Press, 1951.

Haring, Clarence H. "Trade and Navigation between Spain and The Indies: A Re-View—1918–1958." *The Hispanic American Historical Review,* vol. 40, no. 1 (1960), pp. 53–62.

Lockhart, James. "Encomienda and Hacienda: The Evolution of the Great Estate in the Spanish Indies." *The Hispanic American Historical Review,* vol. 49, no. 3 (1969), pp. 411–429.

MacLeod, Murdo. *Spanish Central America. A Socioeconomic History, 1520–1720.* Berkeley: University of California Press, 1973.

*Prado, Caio, Jr. *The Colonial Background of Modern Brazil.* Berkeley: University of California Press, 1967.

Rich, E. E., and Wilson, C. H. (eds.). *The Economy of Expanding Europe in the Sixteenth and Seventeenth Centuries. The Cambridge Economic History of Europe,* vol. 4. Cambridge: Cambridge University Press, 1967.

Simpson, Lesley Byrd. *The Encomienda in New Spain,* rev. ed. Berkeley: University of California Press, 1950.

*Stein, Stanley, J., and Barbara H. *The Colonial Heritage of Latin America. Essays on Economic Dependence in Perspective.* New York: Oxford University Press, 1970.

Taylor, William B. *Landlord and Peasant in Colonial Oaxaca.* Stanford: Stanford University Press, 1972.

**CHAPTER 3**

Borah, Woodrow. "Social Welfare and Social Obligation in New Spain: A Tentative Assessment." *Actas del XXXVI Congreso Internacional de Americanistas,* vol. 4: 45–57. Sevilla: XXXVI Congreso Internacional de Americanistas, 1966.

*Chevalier, François. *Land and Society in Colonial Mexico: The Great Hacienda.* Berkeley: University of California Press, 1963.

Cook, Sherburne F., and Borah, Woodrow. *Essays in Population History: Mexico and the Caribbean,* vol. 1. Berkeley: University of California Press, 1971.

Curtin, Philip D. *The Atlantic Slave Trade: A Census.* Madison: University of Wisconsin Press, 1969.

Gibson, Charles. *The Aztecs Under Spanish Rule: A History of the Indians of the Valley of Mexico, 1519–1810*. Stanford: Stanford University Press, 1964.

Keith, Robert G. "Encomienda, Hacienda and Corregimiento in Spanish America: A Structural Analysis." *The Hispanic American Historical Review*, vol. 51, no. 3 (1971), pp. 431–446.

Kubler, George. "The Quechua in the Colonial World." Julian Steward (ed.), *Handbook of South American Indians*, vol. 2: 331–410. Washington, D.C.: Smithsonian Institution, 1946.

Lockhart, James. "The Social History of Colonial Spanish America: Evolution and Potential." *Latin American Research Review*, vol. 6, no. 1 (1972), pp. 6–45.

*Mörner, Magnus. *Race Mixture in the History of Latin America*. Boston: Little, Brown & Co., 1967.

Morse, Richard M. "Trends and Issues in Latin American Urban Research." *Latin American Research Review*, vol. 6, no. 1 (1971), pp. 3–52 and no. 2 (1971), pp. 19–75.

## CHAPTER 4

Friede, Juan, and Keen, Benjamin (eds.). *Bartolomé de Las Casas in History: Toward an Understanding of the Man and His Work*. Dekalb: Northern Illinois University Press, 1972.

*Hanke, Lewis. *The Spanish Struggle for Justice in the Conquest of America*. Boston: Little, Brown & Co., 1965 (reprint).

*Haring, Clarence H. *The Spanish Empire in America*. New York: Harcourt Brace Jovanovich, Inc., 1963.

Parry, J. H. *The Sale of Public Office in the Spanish Indies Under the Hapsburgs*. Ibero-Americana, vol. 37. Berkeley: University of California Press. 1953.

Phelan, John L. *The Kingdom of Quito in the Seventeenth Century: Bureaucratic Politics in the Spanish Empire*. Madison: University of Wisconsin Press, 1967.

Ricard, Robert. *The Spiritual Conquest of Mexico*. Berkeley: University of California Press, 1966.

———. "Comparison of Evangelization in Portuguese and Spanish America." *The Americas* (Washington, D.C.), vol. 14, no. 4 (1958), pp. 109–117.

## CHAPTER 5

Arciniegas, Germán. *Latin America: A Cultural History*. New York: Alfred A. Knopf, Inc., 1967.

Boxer, Charles R. *The Dutch Seaborne Empire: 1600–1800*. New York: Alfred A. Knopf, Inc., 1965.

*Elliott, J. H. *The Old World and the New, 1492–1650*. Cambridge: Cambridge University Press, 1970.

*Jensen, De Lamar (ed.). *The Expansion of Europe: Motives, Methods, and Meanings.* Problems in European Civilization. Boston: Heath & Co., 1967.

O'Gorman, Edmundo. *The Invention of America: An Inquiry into the Historical Nature of the New World and the Meaning of Its History.* Bloomington: Indiana University Press, 1961.

Parry, J. H., and Sherlock, P. M. *A Short History of the West Indies.* London: Macmillan & Co., 1956.

*Picón Salas, Mariano. *A Cultural History of Spanish America: From Conquest to Independence.* Berkeley: University of California Press, 1962.

Webb, Walter P. *The Great Frontier.* Boston: Houghton Mifflin Co., 1952.

# Chronology

1563   Huancavelica mercury mine discovered in Peru.

1565   *Corregidores de indios* established in Peru. First crossing of the Pacific from the Philippines to New Spain.

1567   The Duke of Alba and his troops arrive in the Netherlands.

1568   Philip II imposes censorship of books and forbids Spaniards to study in foreign universities.

1570–1603   *Pueblos de indios* established in Peru and New Spain.

1574   Reforms of the Council of Trent begin to be applied in Spanish America.

1580   Philip II becomes king of Portugal.

1589   José de Acosta obtains permission to publish his *Natural and Moral History of the Indies.*

1591   Royal decree regulating appropriations of "vacant lands" in Spanish America.

1591–1600   Peak of legal American silver exports to Seville.

1592, 1613   Merchants' guilds established in Mexico City and Lima, respectively.

1594   Embargo of traffic between Iberian and Dutch ports.

1596   Treaty of The Hague: Holland, England, and France allied against the Spanish monarchy.

1602   The Dutch East India Company established.

1604–1605   Hugo Grotius writes a treatise, part of which is published under the title *Mare Liberum.*

1609   The Twelve Years' Truce: practical independence of Holland.

1609, 1614   The Amsterdam Exchange Bank and the Loan Bank, respectively, established in Holland.

1621   The Dutch West India Company established.

1628   First Spanish silver fleet captured by the Dutch.

1629–1660   Peak of Brazilian sugar exports.

1630–1654   The Dutch in Brazil.

1634   Curaçao occupied by the Dutch.

1638, 1641   Elmina and Luanda, respectively, taken by the Dutch.

1640   The great internal crisis of the Spanish monarchy. Rebellion and subsequent independence of Portugal.

1651   English Navigation Acts.

1652–1654   First Anglo-Dutch war.

1655   English occupation of Jamaica.

# Glossary

| | |
|---:|:---|
| *audiencia* | A high court of justice in territories of the Spanish Monarchy. |
| *bandeira* | The Portuguese counterpart in Brazil of the Spanish *compaña*. |
| *bandeirante* | An explorer or raider, member of a *bandeira* in Brazil. |
| *baquiano* | Old Spanish for a veteran, experienced raider, or settler familiarized with the Caribbean scene. |
| *caballería* | A large tract of land granted to a horseman as a reward for his services during the Spanish conquest, or later granted to a resident of a Spanish city in the New World. |
| *cabildo* | The town council of a Spanish colonial city. |
| cacique | A local Indian chieftain in the Caribbean region. |
| *capitulación* | A written agreement between the king of Castile and one of his subjects for purposes of overseas trade, exploration, or conquest. |
| *Casa de Contratación* | The royal board of colonial trade established in Seville. |
| *compaña or compañía* | Old Spanish for a band of business partners, organized as a military company, involved in raiding, slavehunting, exploration, or conquest. |
| *Consejo de Indias* | The top administrative, judicial, fiscal, and governing body for the colonies, established in the Spanish court. |
| *Conselho Ultramarino* | The overseas council established in Lisbon, with authority over all the Portuguese colonies. |
| *corregidor (de españoles)* | A Royal officer ruling a province or large colonial district with a Spanish population. |
| *corregidor de indios* | A royal officer administering a colonial rural district inhabited by Indians. |
| corregimiento | The territory administered by any corregidor. |
| Cortes | A parliamentary Spanish institution of medieval origin. |
| criollo/criolla | Man/woman of supposedly white origin but born in the New World. |
| *curaca* | A local Indian chieftain in colonial Peru. |
| encomienda | The institution under which a number of Indians were entrusted to a Spanish colonist, who could exact from them labor service. Later on he could obtain from them only a specified amount of tribute in cash. |

*encomendero*  The holder of an encomienda.

*engenho de açucar*  Portuguese for sugar mill. By extension, the whole sugar plantation was called *engenho* in Brazil.

fazenda  The late Portuguese counterpart of the Spanish hacienda.

*feitoria*  Portuguese for Old English "factory," a usually fortified coastal trading settlement overseas.

*hacendado*  The owner of a hacienda.

hacienda  A large rural estate in the Spanish colonies.

*indiano*  Spanish for a man coming back rich from the New World.

*ingenio azucarero*  Old Spanish for sugar mill. By extension, the entire sugar plantation was called *ingenio* in Spanish America.

*mayorazgo*  An entail. The legal practice of settling property inalienability on the eldest son of a family in each generation.

*mercader*  A wealthy wholesale merchant.

mestizo  In colonial Spanish America, a half-breed of Spaniard and Indian.

*mita*  The Quechua word for shift. In Spanish Peru, *mita* was the draft system which provided the mines with forced but paid Indian manpower.

*oidor*  The Senior Crown judge serving in an *audiencia*.

paisano  A man from one's own home town.

*Padroado*  Royal Patronage, which gave to the king of Portugal authority over the clergy and privileges in ecclesiastical matters.

*Patronato Real*  The Spanish counterpart of the Portuguese *Padroado*.

peon  A foot soldier.

*peonía*  A small tract of land granted to a foot soldier as a reward for his services in the Spanish conquest, or later granted to a resident of a Spanish city in the New World.

peso  A Spanish colonial silver coin.

*pueblo de indios*  A colonial Indian village or small town.

*senado da camara*  The Portuguese counterpart of the Spanish *cabildo*.

*senhor de engenho*  The owner of a sugar plantation in Brazil.

# Index

**A NOTE**
**ON THE TYPE**

This book is set in Electra, a Linotype face designed by W. A. Dwiggins. This face cannot be classified as either modern or old-style. It is not based on any historical model, nor does it echo any particular period or style. It avoids the extreme contrasts between thick and thin elements that mark most modern faces, and attempts to give a feeling of fluidity, power, and speed.

Composed by Cherry Hill Composition, Pennsauken, New Jersey. Printed and bound by Bookcrafters, Inc., Fredericksburg, Virginia.